Septuagint:

Joshua

Septuagint, Volume 6

SCRIPTURAL RESEARCH INSTITUTE
Published by Digital Ink Productions, 2024

Copyright

Septuagint: Joshua

Second edition. February 19, 2024

Copyright © 2024 Scriptural Research Institute.

ISBN: 978-1-998288-46-5

The Septuagint was translated into Greek at the Library of Alexandria between 250 and 132 BC.

This English translation was created by the Scriptural Research Institute in 2019 and 2020, primarily from the Codex Vaticanus, although the Codex Alexandrinus was also used for reference. Additionally, the Leningrad Codex and Aleppo Codex of the Masoretic Text, the Targum Jerusalem, and Dead Sea Scrolls 4QJosh[a], and 4QJosh[b] were used for comparative analysis.

The image used for the cover is 'Joshua Commanding the Sun to Stand Still' by John Martin, painted in 1840. The original painting is located in the Yale Center for British Art, in New Haven.

Table of Contents

TABLE OF CONTENTS

TABLE OF CONTENTS

Forward

In the mid 3rd century BC, King Ptolemy II Philadelphus of Egypt ordered a translation of the ancient Israelite scriptures for the Library of Alexandria. This translation later became known as the Septuagint, based on the description of the translation by seventy translators in the Letter of Aristeas. The original version, published circa 250 BC, only included the Torah, or in Greek terms, the Pentateuch. The Torah is the five books traditionally credited to Moses, circa 1500 BC: Cosmic Genesis, Exodus, Leviticus, Numbers, and Deuteronomy. According to Jewish tradition, the original Torah was lost when the Babylonians destroyed the Temple of Solomon, and it was then rewritten by Ezra the Scribe from memory during the Second Temple period.

The first edition was followed by the second, around 225 BC which added the books of Joshua, Judges, and Ruth, which was later known as the Octateuch. This version of the Septuagint was later carried south into the Kingdom of Kush by the Israelites fleeing Egypt in 200 BC when Judea was in revolt and the Ptolemys attempted to exterminate the Israelites in Egypt. The Octateuch later became the Torah of the Beta Israel community in Sudan and Ethiopia known as the Orit.

1

It is generally accepted that there were several versions written in Phoenician or Aramaic before the translation of the Septuagint. Fragments of the book of Joshua have been found among the dead sea scrolls, however, only in the Assyrian script of the Herodian Dynasty, and dated to between 37 BC and 6 AD. By this time, the land of Judea passed from the rule of the Ptolemys in Egypt to the rule of the Seleucids in Syria in 200 BC. The Seleucids attempted to Hellenize the Judeans, and effectively banned traditional Judaism. This Hellenizing activity was partially successful, creating the Sadducee faction of Judaism, however also led to the Maccabean Revolt in 165 BC, which itself created the independent Hasmonean Kingdom of Judea. This kingdom was violently xenophobic and led by a priestly monarchy that combined both the powers of the state and the church.

The Hasmonean dynasty attempted to conquer all of the territory that had previously been part of the Persian Province of Judea, and either evicted or exterminated the people that were living there, depending on their ethnicity. When the Edomites were conquered they were allowed to mass-convert to Judaism as they were considered the descendants of Esau, however, most other ethnic groups were not welcome. When the army of Hasmonean King John Hyrcanus annexed Samaria in 113

BC, he slaughtered the Samaritan priests and more than half the Samaritan population and enslaved the rest. His army also destroyed the Samaritan Temple on Mount Gerizim and burned all copies of their holy books. The Samaritans continued to be slaves under the Hasmoneans until the Roman General Pompey's armies freed them in 69 BC, and restored the independent state of Samaria, along with several other states that fell under Rome's protection from that time forward.

While the Hasmoneans ruled Judea, they converted the national script from the old Canaanite script, today called Paleo-Hebrew, to the Assyrian 'block script,' today called Hebrew. As a result, almost all surviving texts found from the Hasmonean era and later are written in the Assyrian script, and it is unclear how much the Hasmoneans redacted the scriptures when they transcribed them. The scriptures the Hasmoneans left the world were later used as the basis of the Masoretic Text, which is used today by Rabbinical Jews, as well as by Catholic and Protestant Christians. The Samaritan Torah is believed to have been restored after General Pompey freed the Samaritans, by redacting a copy of the Hasmonean Torah, which is why there are fewer differences between the Samaritan and Jewish (Masoretic) Torahs than either of them and the Septuagint. A copy of the original Samaritan Torah was translated at the

Library of Alexandria as well, referred to as the Samareitikon (Σαμαρειτικον), however, it has not survived to the present. Based on the writings of Origen of Alexandria in the early 3rd century, and other early Christians, the Samareitikon was more similar to the Septuagint's Pentateuch than it was to either the Samaritan or Jewish Torahs in use at the time.

The differences between the Masoretic and the Septuagint's version of Joshua, and several other books in the two collections of scriptures are both minor and startling, as the two sets of scriptures contain the same stories, but different Gods. The God of the book of Joshua in the Septuagint is called Lord the God (Κύριοσ ὁ θεὸσ) or simplified to Lord (Κύριοσ), or God (Θεὸσ). These terms are mirrored in the Masoretic version of Joshua with Yehvah your god (יְהוָה אֱלֹהֶיךָ), Yhwh my god (יהוה אלהי), and Yehvah (יְהוָה). One explanation for the difference between the texts is the Christian redaction of the 3rd century AD, when the name Iaô (Ιαω) was removed from the Septuagint, replaced by Lord (Κύριοσ). Fragments of older Septuagint manuscripts still exist that contain the name Iaô (Ιαω), transliterated from the Aramaic Yhw (יה^), however, none of the fragments of the Book of Joshua include the name. The name Yhwh (יהוה) is found in a couple of fragments of Joshua found among the Dead Sea Scrolls, however, both date to the Herodian dynasty, and therefore date to over 185 years after the Septuagint's version of Joshua was translated.

The Aramaic sections of Masoretic Daniel that were not translated into Hebrew maintain the term adonai ha'elohim (אֲדֹנָי הָאֱלֹהִים), meaning the 'Lord the gods' where the Septuagint has 'Lord the god' (Κύριον τὸν θεὸν), however, the Hebrew sections have Yehvah elohim (יְהוָה אֱלֹהִים) where the Septuagint has 'Lord the god,' suggesting the Greek more accurately reflects the Aramaic source texts than the Hebrew translation. According to some records from the time, this was to repair the damage King Manasseh had done 600 years earlier when he removed the name Yhwh from the Israelite Texts, however, no evidence has survived from the era of Manasseh or earlier that proves the name was originally in the text, suggesting it was an attempt by the first Hasmonean High-Priest/King Simon the Zealot to create a national Judean religion with a god having a name similar to the Roman god Jove.

The Greek terms in the Septuagint's Joshua are translations of well-known terms related to Canaanite god El, the Canaanite creator-god. El translates in Canaanite, Aramaic, and Hebrew as 'God,' and was the primary god worshiped in ancient Canaan in the era Abraham, Isaac, and Jacob were reported to have passed through the area.

El was also the patron god of the Temple of El, built by Jacob near the modern city of Nablus in the Palestinian West Bank, which featured in many of the early Hebrew scriptures before Samaria was conquered by the Assyrian Empire. In the Book of Micah, the Temple of El was referred to as Jacob's Temple of El, which confirms that the Israelites in the 8th century BC considered the Temple of El at Shiloh to be the Temple of El that Jacob built, in Genesis chapter 35.

The Septuagint's book of Joshua also has the first reference to Sabaoth (Σαβαωθ) in chapter 6, as Lord Sabaoth (Κυρίω Σαβαωθ). Lord Sabaoth was the Judahite God during the rule of the Greeks, whom the Greeks equated with Dionysus, and the Romans equated with Bacchus. In Aramaic, the language which was spoken in Judea during the Persian and Greek eras, ådny Ṣbå (אדני צבא) meant 'lord of desires,' however, when the Hasmonean Dynasty seized control of Judea and made the newly invented 'ancient' Hebrew language official, they changed the meaning of the word to 'military' or 'army,' making the Lord of Desires into the Lord of War.

The Torah appears to have been redacted by the Hasmonean Dynasty circa 140 BC, when it was translated into Hebrew, in an attempt to forge closer ties with Rome, which was still a distant power across the Mediterranean, outside of Greek domination. As the

Maccabean Revolt raged against Greek rule in Judea, between 165 and 140 BC, the Romans were fighting the final, and bloodiest of their wars against the Carthaginians, the ancient Canaanite colony base in modern Tunisia. The Carthaginians were once the great power of the Western Mediterranean, dominating north-west Africa, southern and western Iberia, Sicily, Sardinia, and Corsica.

The Romans had been at almost constant war against Carthage for over a century, beginning with the first Punic war in 264 BC, and in 146 BC finally defeated them, and effectively exterminated the race. Roman records report that they forced the surviving Carthaginian warriors to fight to the death in arenas, while the civilians were sold as slaves to anyone that would buy them. The population of northwest Africa became a slave-race for centuries and was not freed until the rise of Christianity in the 4th century. In 139 BC, seven years after the end of the final Punic war, and the year after the Hasmonean dynasty was established in Judea, the Romans evicted all Jews from the republic because the Jews were attempting to promote the idea that the Roman national god Jupiter (Iovis) was their national god Yahweh Sabaoth (Jupiter Sabazius). This was recorded by Valerius Maximus:

"Gnaeus Cornelius Hispalus, praetor peregrinus in the year of the consulate of Marcus Popilius Laenas and Lucius Calpurnius, ordered the astrologers by an edict to leave Rome and Italy within ten days, since by a fallacious interpretation of the stars they perturbed fickle and silly minds, thereby making profit out of their lies. The same praetor compelled the Jews, who attempted to infect the Roman custom with the cult of Jupiter Sabazius, to return to their homes."

As there had been Judeans living in Rome before 139 BC, and the Romans had interpreted Lord Sabaoth as the Judean version of Dionysus, it is clear something had changed significantly within Judea when the Hasmoneans seized power. The books of the Maccabees, set during the late Greek Era, Maccabean Revolt, and early Hasmonean Dynasty describe Dionysus being worshiped in the Temple in Jerusalem, before the revolution, confirming that the Judeans also considered Lord Sabaoth to be the Judean version of Dionysus. In the Masoretic version of Joshua, the name Lord Sabaoth was entirely replaced by Yhwh (יהוה), indicating that the Masoretic version of Joshua was created after King/High-Priest Simon the Zealot's failed attempt to convert Rome to his religion.

The Hebrew word transliterated as Sabaoth, which the Greeks and Romans treated as the proper name of the Judean god, is a military term, roughly meaning 'army' or 'military.' As such, the fusion of the Hasmonean god Yahweh with Sabaoth created a militaristic version of Yahweh, a war-god, for a warrior-dynasty. The Hasmoneans may have promoted Yahweh Sabaoth, however, in Joshua, Sabaoth is not called Iaw Sabaoth, but Lord Sabaoth. This cannot be as a result of the Christian redaction of the name Iaô (Ιαω) in the 3rd century, as the Masoretic Text only have Yahweh, not Yahweh Sabaoth. Lord Sabaoth is only mentioned once in Joshua, with all other references to Lord the god, the Lord, or God. He was mentioned when the Israelites were preparing to attack Jericho, however, his generalissimo (ἀρχιστράτηγοσ) was introduced clumsily at the end of the previous chapter.

When Joshua was in Jericho, he looked up with his eyes and saw a man standing before him, and there was a drawn sword in his hand, and Joshua approached and said to him, "Are you with us, or on the side of our enemies?"

He answered him, "I have now come, the Generalissimo of the army of the Lord."

Joshua fell on his face to the earth, and said to him, "Lord, what do you command of your servant?"

The Generalissimo of the Lord said to Joshua, "Remove your shoes off your feet, for the place on which you now stand is sacred."

This section of the text does not line up with text the before it or after it. Joshua's people had not attacked Jericho yet, and the Israelites were not in the city. Moreover, if the city was sacred, God should not have destroyed it. This section of text appears to have either been added to the original text, or to be a relic of another, possibly older version of the Jericho story. However it came to be in the book of Joshua, it is in both the Septuagint's and Masoretic version of Joshua, meaning it must have been in the Aramaic version. This generalissimo of the army of the Lord, appears to be Lord Sabaoth, the 'Lord of War' in Canaanite and Hebrew, mentioned in the next chapter, meaning that he was not God, but a soldier sent by the Lord, or a lord, to Jericho, which was apparently sacred to the lord in question. This reference to a Lord other than God is consistent with the early Israelite religion before the reforms of King Josiah circa 625 BC when there were many Lords worshiped in Judah. These reforms are described in detail in the Septuagint's 4th Kingdoms (Masoretic Kings) chapter 23:

> The king commanded Hilkiah the high priest, and the priests of the second order, and them that kept the door, to bring out of the temple of the Lord all the vessels that were made for Ba'al, and for Asherah, and all the army of Shamayim, and he burnt them outside of Jerusalem in the fields of Kidron, and took the ashes of them to the Temple of El. He burnt the sacred male prostitutes, who the kings

of Judah had appointed, and those burnt incense in the Bamahs and in the cities of Judah, and the places around Jerusalem, and those that burnt incense to Ba'al, Shemesh, Yarikh, the Zodiac, and the power of the armies of Shamayim.

He carried out the Asherah from the Temple of the Lord to the brook Kidron, and burnt it at the brook Kidron, and ground it to powder, and threw its powder on the sepulchers of the sons of the people. He pulled down the Palace of Qetesh that were by the Temple of the Lord, where the women wove tents for the Asherah. He brought up all the priests from the cities of Judah and defiled the Bamahs where the priests burnt incense, from Geba even to Beersheba.

He pulled down the house of the gates that were by the door of the gate of Joshua the ruler of the city, on a man's left hand at the gate of the city. The priests of the Bamahs did not go up to the altar of the Lord in Jerusalem, and they only ate leavened bread among their brothers. He defiled Tafeth which is in the valley of the son of Hinns, constructed for a man to cause his son or his daughter to pass through the fire to Moloch. He burnt the horses which the king of Judah had given to Shemesh in the entrance of the Temple of the Lord, by the treasury of Nathan the king's eunuch, in the suburbs, and he burnt the Chariot of Shemesh with fire.

The altars that were on the roof of the upper room of Ahaz, which the kings of Judah had made, and the altars which Manasseh had made in the two courts of the Temple of the Lord, the king pulled down and forcibly removed from there and threw their dust into the Brook of Kidron. The king defiled the temple that was near Jerusalem, on the right hand of the mount of Mosthath, which Solomon king of Israel built to Astarte the abomination of the Sidonians, and to Chemosh the abomination of Moab, and to Moloch the abomination of the Ammanites. He broke in pieces the steles, and completely destroyed Asherah, and filled their places with the bones of men. Also the high altar in the Temple of El, which had been built by Jeroboam the son of Nebat, who made Israel sin, even that high altar he tore down, and broke in pieces the stones of it, and reduced it to powder, and burnt Asherah.

Josiah turned aside, and saw the tombs that were there in the city, and sent, and took the bones out of the tombs, and burnt them on the altar, and defiled it, following the word of the Lord which the prophet spoke...

The reforms that took place in Judah under Josiah were both extreme and lasting, as the god Yahweh continues to be the God of Judaism today. Nevertheless, he has not always been the god of the Judahites. The Septuagint's 1ˢᵗ Ezra recounts how after killing King Josiah, the Pharaoh Necho II restored the worship of the 'Lord' in Judah, which could only be a reference to the sun god Amen, which Necho II is recorded as worshiping in Egyptian records, along with the North Egyptian version of Amen known as Atum. The Septuagint's book of Baruch, written by the scribe Baruch in Babylon after Nebuchadnezzar II had destroyed Jerusalem a couple of decades later, describes his god as the sun, meaning that sun worship had been restored in Judah after Josiah's death. Throughout the subsequent Persian and Greek rules of Judea, several gods were reportedly worshiped in Jerusalem, including Ahura Mazda, the Zoroastrian God, and Lord Sabaoth, who seems to have been very different from the militaristic interpretation of the Hasmonean Yahweh of Armies.

The 'Hebrew' language of the Hasmonean Dynasty, was a reformed version of the southern Canaanite dialect spoken in Judea and Edom, written with a specific form of the Aramaic script that the Judeans called 'Assyrian' in the Talmud. While it was a new language in that the Hasmonean Dynasty appear to have been the first government that attempted to standardize it, it was quite similar to both the surviving forms of Ugaritic Canaanite from the Bronze Age, and Phoenician Canaanite from the Iron Age, meaning other than changing the name and script to something that didn't sound or look too Carthaginian, the language was essentially the same as Bronze Age Canaanite. Therefore, the original reference in Joshua to Lord Sabaoth was probably to a military commander, and not a magic genie, like the Aramaic version appears to have read.

The question of who this military commander was, at Jericho, in 1508 BC according to the Septuagint's chronology is generally ignored by those that assume it was God or a supernatural warrior sent by God, however, it is a matter of record that the army of Thutmose I marched through Canaan in the year 1505 BC, using the standard chronology of Egyptian history, and found no one to fight them. According to the archaeological record, the city of Jericho was destroyed sometime shortly before 1500 BC, and not rebuilt until the Iron Age. It is generally accepted that the Egyptian army destroyed the city, although Thutmose I did not report visiting the city himself, and would have mentioned destroying the city. There is no record of an Egyptian military expedition in 1508 BC, however, Egypt was not the only power at the time interested in Canaan, as between 1540 and 1500 BC the Mitanni Empire was rapidly expanding into northern Canaan. It is possible that the Generalissimo was a Mitanni war-chief.

While many scholars have questioned the age of the Book of Joshua, most of the criticism against it seems misdirected at the Hebrew translation, which must date to sometime between 140 and 37 BC. There are references in Joshua that point to the authorship of Joshua, or at least parts of it, in the Late Bronze Age. Specifically, the treatment of iron. Prior to the Bronze-Age collapse, circa 1200 BC, iron was rare in the Middle East and mainly used for jewelry. This treatment of iron as a valuable metal shows up in Joshua at the Battle of Jericho, when Joshua orders:

> All the silver, or gold, or brass, or iron, will be holy to the Lord. It will be carried into the treasury of the Lord.

Later, however, iron is treated as a common metal used in chariots, indicating that the Book of Joshua was added to later during the iron age, likely in the centuries before King Josiah's time, when the Israelites were worshiping many gods. The reference to the sun and the moon standing still in the sky would have meant something different to the pre-Josiah Israelites, as Shemesh and Yarikh were gods, but were obeying Joshua. As the author put it:

> "The sun and the moon stood still until God executed vengeance on their enemies, and the sun stood still in the middle of the sky. It did not proceed to set until the end of one day. There was not a day like it either before or after, that god should listen to man..."

This places the pre-Hasmonean redaction of Joshua before the time of Josiah, likely when the text was originally translated from cuneiform into Aramaic in the Kingdom of Samaria. The geographical references cover all of Canaan from Egypt to Syria, and so it is not easy to place a geographical origin to the text. It does, however, contradict the books of the Kingdoms, as it has Joshua conquering Jebus (Jerusalem), and not David. This would point to a Samaritan origin, as the Samaritans never accepted the city of Jerusalem as having been the capital of Israel, instead claiming that Shechem, and later the city of Samaria were the capital. If the text was translated into Aramaic in Samaria, this would have been between 930 and 720 BC. Nevertheless, some sections of the text must date back to before the Bronze Age collapse, to explain the value placed on iron.

The longer ending of Joshua is also found in some copies of the Septuagint and is included in this translation. In it, the Israelites turned away from worshiping Lord the god and started worshiping Astarte, Athtart, and the gods of the nations around them, resulting in God withdrawing his protection, and the Israelites being conquered by the Moabites. These two short verses end the book very differently from the Masoretic version, in which the Israelites are, presumably, still worshiping Lord the god, and live happily ever after. The paring of Astarte and Athtart (Ἀστάρτην καὶ Ασταρωθ) also dates the text to the late Bronze Age, as, by the early Iron Age, Astarte and Athtart had merged into the goddess simply called Qetesh, meaning 'holiness.'

The two goddesses mentioned are the wives of El from the Bronze Age Ugaritic Texts: Åṯrt (⯈⥤⟨⊨⯈⥥), later called Asherah (אשרה) by the Israelites; and Ôṭtrt-ym (𐤀𐤔𐤓𐤕𐤌), later called Ôštrt (𐤏𐤔𐤕𐤓𐤕) by the Phoenicians, Astarte (Ἀστάρτη) by the Greeks, and Ashtoret (עַשְׁתֹּרֶת) by the Israelites. The Phoenician Ôštrt (𐤏𐤔𐤕𐤓𐤕) was descended from Ôṭtrt-ym (𐤀𐤔𐤓𐤕𐤌), the sea goddess which also gave rise to Aphrodite, while the Israelite Åšrh (אשרה) was descended from Åṭrt (𐤀𐤔𐤓𐤕), the goddess of the land. In the early Canaanite mythology, the sea and land appear to have been viewed as the two wives of El, the bull in the sky. During the Egyptian New Kingdoms era, which took place at the same time as the events in the books of Joshua and Judges, the two goddesses merged, along with the Egyptian goddess Hathor, into Qetesh, a goddess that assumed the 'sky goddess' role of Hathor, which seems to have been how the Israelites viewed her until King Josiah's reforms of circa 625 BC. This merger of Astarte and Asherah clearly dates the authorship of Joshua to the early New Kingdom Era, circa 1500 BC.

The general view of both historians and biblical scholars is that the Book of Joshua holds no historical value, and is simply a book written during the life of Josiah, or during the Babylonian captivity, or even later by Ezra during the Second Temple Era, however, this is based on analysis of the Masoretic version of the book, which is quite different from the Septuagint's version. In

Rabbinical history, as a century and a half have been redacted, Joshua's life is dated to the early 1300s BC, instead of the late 1500s BC. This era does not align with anything found in the archaeological record, and therefore the book reads like fiction. Likewise, the Masoretic version is about a god named Yahweh, a name not known to archaeology until around 800 BC, meaning that the Book of Joshua, if the Masoretic version were the original, would have to have been written after that time. The Septuagint's version is quite different in the details, as the god of the book is Lord the god, almost certainly a translation of the term ådny ha'elohim found in the Aramaic sections of Daniel, and the title of the god El who the ancient Canaanites were worshiping in the 2nd millennium BC. Joshua's invasion of Canaan circa 1508 BC, 42 years after the Minoan Eruption, would also place the Israelites at Jericho at around the time the walls were torn down.

The ruins of Jericho were identified as the mound at Tell es-Sultan in 1869, and this is still generally accepted as ancient Jericho. The city was a major trading center, and heavily fortified city for thousands of years, until circa 1500 BC when the walls were torn down. The exact date when the walls were torn down is unclear, with estimates ranging from 1700 to 1400 BC, however, 1500 BC is the most widely quoted date.

In approximately 1504 BC the Egyptian King Thutmose I led an expedition through Canaan and Syria to the Euphrates River, and it is assumed by many historians that he ripped down the walls of Jericho, however, that is not possible. Thutmose recorded that he found no one to fight him in Canaan, and the local peoples submitted to Egyptian power without conflict. Moreover, later the same year he launched his invasion of Nubia, to the south of Egypt, meaning he simply did not have time to secretly lay siege to Jericho. This pacified Canaan ruled by people who were afraid of the Egyptians is consistent with the account in Joshua, however, the Egyptian 'invasion' is not mentioned in Joshua. Given the history between the Israelites and Egyptians, it is not unlikely it would have been omitted, especially if there was no war, and the Israelites surrendered to the Egyptians without a fight.

After 1500 BC the people in Canaan, whoever they were, began fortifying their cities. Thutmose I's heir, Thutmose II, also sent an expedition into Canaan and Syria, and crossed the Euphrates, however, only reported fighting nomads in the Sinai. There are no records of his successor, Queen Hatshepsut invading Canaan. Her heir Thutmose III did send multiple armies through Canaan demanding tribute, however, these campaigns appear to have been mostly peaceful until around 1450 BC, when he marched his army into northern Canaan to invade Syria and occupied all of Canaan in the process. The cities of Kadesh on the Orontes (in modern Syria), and Byblos in modern Lebanon, are mentioned as being major conquests of his campaigns, which laid the foundation for his later attack on the Mitanni Empire in Syria.

After Thutmose's campaign, the region was formally part of the Egyptian Empire for centuries, however, Egyptian records show they generally left the people alone and did not exert much control over the region beyond demanding regular tribute. The Egyptian records show there were many local chieftains during this era, sometimes fighting each other, or a people called the Habiru, which some believe to be an ancient reference to the Hebrews. This era of nominal Egyptian occupation would be the era of the Judges when the Israelites had no king. Obviously, if they did not have a king, they were a subjugated people.

Supporters of the earlier dating for the tearing down of Jericho's walls, generally assume the Hyksos dynasty ripped them down at some point, and as there are few records from the era, it cannot be proven or disproven. Nevertheless, after the walls were ripped down the site was reoccupied briefly, and a small town was present at the ruins until circa 1500 BC, in the dating when the walls were ripped down between 1700 and 1600 BC. In the dating when the walls were ripped down circa 1500, this village existed until circa 1400 BC. In either event, the village was destroyed by someone. If the earlier dating for the walls being torn down is correct, then the walls were already torn down when Joshua's army arrived, and they simply destroyed a small unfortified settlement in the ruins of the ancient city. In that scenario, the story about the walls falling when the Israelites shouted at them was a later fictional element added at some point. However, in either case, whether the Israelites tore down the walls or not, a city or village was destroyed at Jericho circa 1500 BC, according to the archaeological evidence, supporting both the dating of the Minoan eruption in Exodus, and the invasion of Canaan by the Israelites right before the Egyptians occupied the region.

The Israelite invasion of Canaan circa 1508 BC could have been as one-sided as the Book of Joshua depicts it, as the region was divided among many petty 'kings' that emerged from the collapse of the Hyksos Dynasty circa 1540 BC, when their last fortified city, Sharuhen, fell to the armies of Pharaoh Ahmose I. The siege of Sharuhen took the Egyptian army three years, and it was significantly smaller than the ancient fortified city of Jericho, proving Thutmose I could not have leveled Jericho in a few weeks. Between 1540 BC, when Sharuhen fell, and 1450 BC, when Thutmose III formally annexed Canaan into his empire in prelude to his invasion of the Mitanni Empire, the region was in chaos by all accounts, and any resistance the Israelites would have encountered circa 1508 BC would have been minimal and unorganized. The kings they fought would have been in power for less than 40 years, and likely had little control over their dominions.

The Egyptian records report the region was divided among many tribes when they passed through the region in 1504 BC, which, does support the idea that there were 12 autonomous tribes at the time, along with subjugated Hurrians and Canaanites, as described in the Book of Joshua. Some of the names of the tribes are archaeologically attested, such as Dan and Gad, however, most are not, leading to speculation that they may have been later inventions. However, the Egyptians did not have consistent and universal names for countries. For example, the Egyptians called the Mitanni kingdom Naharin, Maryannu, and Mitanni. Naharin is believed to have been adopted from the Akkadian word for 'river,' making it a geographical name. In this case, it appears an Egyptian asked a local what the river was called, and applied the word 'river' to the entire land. This would make sense to an Egyptian, as the Nile was the only river in Egypt. The name Maryannu is derived from the name of the Indo-Aryan rulers of the Mitanni Empire, known as 'marya' in Mitanni-Aryan, which translates as 'warrior' in Sanskrit. This was the political name of the land, which would have made sense to someone addressing a Pharaoh, as Egypt was his land. The name Mitanni, or 'me-ta-ni' in ancient Egyptian, appears to be a direct transliteration of the local name, however, was the rarest name they used for the land. Therefore, there is no reason to assume the Israelites were either present in Canaan or absent from Canaan, based on the Egyptian records.

Based on the various references to the Israelites worshiping Baʻal, Asherah, Shamayim, Shemesh, Yarikh, and many other Canaanite gods found in the books of Joshua, Judges, and the books of the Kingdoms, as well as the books of the prophets, it is unlikely the Egyptians would have been able to distinguish them from the Canaanites. Modern archaeologists cannot. Until the era of Josiah, the Israelites appear to have been no different from the Canaanites they supposedly conquered, and most archaeologists doubt there was an invasion. There was the well-documented pillaging of the Habiru, recorded in hundreds of surviving documents from the 2nd millennium BC, by the Canaanites, Egyptians, Akkadians, and Sumerians. These people started out in Sumer and were described as a group of Aramaean nomads that attacked undefended villages and plundered the countryside. Between 1800 and 1200 BC, they lived outside of the major Empires and pillaged the outskirts of Sumer, Akkadia, Babylonia, Assyria, and Canaan.

They were generally described as being murderers and thieves, however, also worked as mercenaries. Based on the Tikunani Prism from around 1550 BC, the majority were Hurrian at the time, although Semitic names were the second most common. In later centuries Indo-Aryan names appeared among them, likely of Mitanni origin. Many have tried to link the history of the Habiru to the Hebrews, and while the names may be connected, there is no evidence of the Habiru having a common god, tribe, or goal. They operated as 'land pirates' marauding their way across the Middle East.

In the Amarna Letters, from circa 1350 BC, the warlord Labaya, the ruler of Shechem, one of Egypt's petty kingdoms, hired Habiru as mercenaries and allowed them to settle in Shechem, meaning that if the Israelites were settled in Shechem by that time, they were not the Habiru. These Habiru settlers did nevertheless contribute to the developing Israelite identity and would have been part of the United Kingdom of Israel if it existed, and the later Kingdom of Samaria. In the Torah, the Israelites were a subset of Hebrews, as

Abraham was a Hebrew, however, only the descendants of Jacob were Israelites. It is plausible that the Israelites were a group of Habiru that settled in Egypt under the Hyksos, however, it is equally plausible the name Hebrew was added to the Torah during Josiah's redaction.

The Book of Joshua is itself a continuation of the story found in Numbers and Deuteronomy, themselves both continuations of the story found in Exodus. Specifically, it appears to be a direct continuation of Deuteronomy, which it may have originally been part of, as the closing verses of Deuteronomy and opening verses of Joshua fit together seamlessly.

So Moses the servant of the Lord died in the land of Moab by the word of the Lord. They buried him in Gai near the Temple of Peor, and no one has seen his sepulcher to this day. Moses was a hundred and twenty years old at his death, yet his eyes were not dimmed, nor were his natural powers destroyed. The children of Israel wept for Moses in Araboth of Moab at the Jordan near Jericho for thirty days, and the days of the sad mourning for Moses were completed.

Joshua the son of Nun was filled with the spirit of knowledge, for Moses had laid his hands on him, and the children of Israel listened to him, and they did as the Lord commanded Moses. There did not rise another prophet in Israel like Moses, whom the Lord knew face to face, in all the signs and wonders, which the Lord sent him to work in Egypt against Pharaoh and his servants and all his land, and the great wonders, and the mighty hand which Moses displayed before all Israel.

After the death of Moses, the Lord said to Joshua the son of Nun, the minister of Moses, "Moses my servant is dead. Now then rise, go across the Jordan, you and all these people, into the land which I give them. Every place on which you will step I will give to you, as I told Moses. The wilderness and Anti-Lebanon, as far as the great river, the river Euphrates, and as far as the farthest sea, your coasts will be at the setting of the sun. Not a man will stand against you all the days of your life, and as I was with Moses, so will I also be with you, and I will not fail you, or neglect you. Be strong and act like a man, as you will divide the land among these people, which I swore to give to your fathers. Be strong, therefore, and act like a man, and observe and do as Moses my servant commanded you. You will not turn from them to the right hand or the left, that you may be wise in whatever you may do. The book of this law will not leave out of your mouth, and you will meditate on it day and night, that you may know how to do all the things that are written in it. Then you will prosper, and make your ways prosperous, and then you will be wise. Look! I have commanded you 'Be strong and courageous, do not be cowardly nor fearful, for Lord the god is with you in all places, to wherever you go.'"

> Joshua commanded the scribes of the people, "Go into the middle of the camp of the people, and command the people, 'Prepare provisions, for in three days you will go across the Jordan, enter into and take possession of the land, which Lord the god of your fathers gives to you."

Joshua also restates the division of the land of Canaan between the twelve tribes, which is previously covered in Numbers but goes into much more depth, stipulating the exact borders of the tribes. This implies that Joshua may have been one of the sources that the Levites used when they cobbled together Numbers for King Josiah. The fact that Deuteronomy and Joshua fit together so seamlessly, indicates it was likely compiled into its pre-Hasmonean form in the Kingdom of Samaria, where Deuteronomy almost certainly originated. Several factors support the book as pre-Josiah and likely ignored entirely by Josiah's reforms, most especially the references to the sun (Shemesh) and moon (Yarikh) obeying Joshua, or possibly Lord the god, depending on interpretation. After Josiah's reforms, the sun and moon were just the sun and moon, two big lights up in the sky that could not listen to anyone. Before his reforms, they were two of the most powerful gods, Shemesh and Yarikh. Certainly, he would not have allowed the heretical implication that they were hearing and thinking and choosing to obey anyone.

The Book of Joshua has traditionally been very unpopular, both with Jews and Christians, and only 3 copies have been found to date among the Dead Sea Scrolls, compared to 22 for Genesis, 17 for Exodus, 15 for Leviticus, 13 for Numbers, and 33 for Deuteronomy. Even Judges and Ruth were more popular with 4 copies of each discovered among the Dead Sea Scrolls. This unpopularity is generally attributed to the 'heroic' genocidal warfare described, which is the antithesis of Christianity and modern Judaism. Many Christian denominations issue advisories for members reading Joshua, printed directly in their bibles, to 'not take the history seriously,' 'it did not happen,' and to 'focus on the spiritual message.' However, there is little spiritual in the book, other than the first appearance of Lord Sabaoth, who became Yahweh Sabaoth in the Hasmonean redaction.

While the Hasmoneans may have tried to court Rome and the rebels in Phrygia and Assyria, there is little evidence that anyone other than the Assyrians was interested in allying with them. A series of wars including both Julius Caesar's campaigns, and a Parthian invasion led to the weakening of the Hasmonean dynasty, and in 37 AD, the Roman Senate appointed Herod the Great as King of the Jews. Herod's rule wasn't particularly popular, as he allowed the Romans to establish themselves within Judea, however, he did expand Judea, reintegrating the Greek and Samaritan cities, and annexing Galilee and Edom. When he died, his kingdom was divided between four successors, a situation that ended in 66 AD when the Romans conquered the region. An uprising in 120 AD led to the Jews being exiled from Judea, and the region became a Greco-Roman colony. In the wake of the Jews, the Samaritans rose in numbers, along with the Christians once Christianity was legalized. Between 529 and 555 AD, the Samaritans revolted and were effectively annihilated, by Constantinople the Eastern Roman capital.

The modern Samaritan religion is similar to Judaism, in that they have versions of the Torah and the book of Joshua, however, they do not trace their ancestry to ancient Judah, but rather to ancient Samaria also called the Northern Kingdom of Israel. According to the Samaritans, they were the original Israelites, and the Temple of the Lord was not Solomon's Temple in Jerusalem, but rather a Temple of Mount Gerizim, in Samaria. These other Israelites also contributed to the creation of the Septuagint, as the Book of Tobit, was the story of a Samaritan that had been taken to Nineveh, the capital of the Assyrian Empire after the Kingdom of Israel was conquered by the Assyrians. This book and several others were not considered important to Simon the Zealot, and not translated into Hebrew.

Outside of Judea, the Septuagint was the dominant form of Israelite scriptures across the Greek-speaking world, which at the beginning of the Christian era extended from the Roman Empire in the west, to the Indo-Greek Kingdom in the east. Judean traders had established small colonies along the trade routes of the Red Sea and the Indian Ocean, reaching as far south as Eritrea, and as far east as southern India, and these Judeans spoke Aramaic and Greek and used the Septuagint. The earliest Christians used the Septuagint exclusively, as far as the Israelite scriptures were concerned, and as a result, it is impossible to even understand the chronology of the world they described unless using the Septuagint. It is unclear why the Septuagint, Masoretic Text, and Samaritan Asatir each contain a different chronology of the world. Adding the Book of Jubilees, and various variations of the Torah found within the Dead Sea Scrolls, there are no less than six ancient Israelite chronologies.

The Septuagint's Genesis includes an additional millennium of human history that was dropped from the Proto-Masoretic Texts in order to align the creation of the world with the beginning of the age of El, when the constellation Taurus became the marker of the northern vernal equinox, in 3760 BC. The Bull El was the dominant God of the Canaanite pantheon until circa 1700 BC, when Attar the Goat (Aries) and Yam the Sea-Monster (Cetus) fought for domination of the world beneath the sky, ultimately both being replaced by the god of thunder Ba'al Hadad, in the Canaanite Ba'al Cycle. Traditional Jewish interpretations of the timeline within the Masoretic Text, is further hampered by the so-called 'missing years' of Rabbinical Time, in which hundreds of years of the Persian Empire are skipped over in order to make the timeline fit into the era since 3760 BC, a problem Christian chronologists have never had as Christianity developed after the astrology of Babylonian-era Judaism had been forgotten.

The earliest Christian Bibles all used the Septuagint, however, by the 4th century some Christian scholars were debating whether they should retranslate the Old Testament from the version the Jews were using, and some even suggested using the Samaritan version. Both suggestions were generally dismissed as heretical, as Jesus and the Apostles had quoted from the Septuagint, even though they had access to the Hebrew version then in use. This argument held in the west until the Middle Ages, when Catholic Bibles switched to the Masoretic Text.

In the east, Orthodox Bibles continued to use the Septuagint, as they do today. To the south, the Ethiopian Tewahedo Church continued to use the Septuagint, and across Asia, the Thomas Christians and Nestorians continued to use the Septuagint. Only in Western Europe were the later Masoretic Text adopted, abandoning the more ancient Septuagint, on the assumption that the Jews had copied their texts more faithfully than the Greeks had translated them. This assumption was carried forward into the Protestant Churches that broke off from the Catholic Church, and therefore almost all Protestant Bibles use the Masoretic Text for the basis of the Old Testament.

Unfortunately, this means that the earliest Christian writings are generally confusing and ignored by Protestants and Catholics. The earliest Christians of the first and second centuries quoted books that are no longer in the Bible, and as such, their writings are not always understood. Septuagint: Joshua is part of a series of 21st century translations aimed at correcting this problem.

One of the problems with academic translations of the Septuagint, is the use of unfamiliar names or terms, as the Septuagint was written in Greek, and therefore many names are unrecognizable to modern readers who are used to Hebrew-derived names. This project uses the more commonly understood Hebrew-derived names instead of their Greek translations, such as Canaan instead of Chanaan, and Melchizedek instead of Melchisedec. Common modern names are also used instead of either Greek or Hebrew terms when geographical locations are known, such as the archaeological name Uruk instead of the Greek Orech, or the Hebrew Erech, and the archaeological term Sumer instead of Shinar or Senar. While this could be argued as not being a correct academic procedure, it does fulfill the goal of making the translation easy to read and understand.

Chapter 1

After the death of Moses, the Lord[1] said to Joshua the son of Nun, the minister of Moses, "Moses my servant is dead. Now then rise, go across the Jordan, you and all these people, into the land which I give them. Every place on which you will step I will give to you, as I told Moses. The wilderness and Anti-Lebanon, as far as the great river, the river Euphrates, and as far as the farthest sea, your coasts will be at the setting of the sun. Not a man will stand against you all the days of your life, and as I was with Moses, so will I also be with you, and I will not fail you, or neglect you. Be strong and act like a man, as you will divide the land among these people, which I swore to give to your fathers."

"Be strong, therefore, and act like a man, and observe and do as Moses my servant commanded you. You will not turn from them to the right hand or the left, that you may be wise in whatever you may do. The book of this law will not leave out of your mouth, and you will meditate on it day and night, that you may know how to do all the things that are written in it. Then you will prosper, and make your ways prosperous, and then you will be wise. Look! I have commanded you 'Be strong and courageous, do not be cowardly nor fearful, for Lord the god[2] is with you in all places, to wherever you go.'"

CHAPTER 1

Joshua commanded the scribes of the people, "Go into the middle of the camp of the people, and command the people, 'Prepare provisions, for in three days you will go across the Jordan, enter into and take possession of the land, which Lord the god of your fathers gives to you."

To Reuben, and to Gad, and to the half-tribe of Manasseh, Joshua said, "Remember the words that Moses the servant of the Lord commanded you, 'The Lord the god has caused you to peace, and has given you this land. Let your wives and your children and your livestock live in the land which he has given you, but you will cross well-armed before your brothers, every one of you who is strong, and you will fight on their side, until Lord the god has given your brothers peace, like you, and they have inherited the land that Lord the god gives them. Then you will leave, each one to his inheritance that Moses gave you to the east of the Jordan."

They answered Joshua, "We will do all things which you command us, and we will go everywhere you will send us. As we listened to Moses, we will listen to you. Only let Lord the god be with you, as he was with Moses. Whoever will disobey you, and whoever will not listen to your words as you will command him, let him die, but you be strong and courageous."

Chapter 1 Notes

1 Codex Vaticanus: c̄s (ⲕⲥ). Translation: lord

- Aleppo Codex: Yhwh (**יהוה**)

- Leningrad Codex: Yehvah (יְהָוֶה)

- Targum Jerusalem: Yeyah (??. Translation: Yahw

This verse does not survive in the Dead Sea Scrolls, however, the name does show up in later verses that have survived.

- Dead Sea Scroll 4QJosh^a: Yhwh (𐤉𐤄𐤅𐤄)

- Dead Sea Scroll 4QJosh^b: Yhwh (𐤉𐤄𐤅𐤄)

The Septuagint's version of the Joshua was translated before 200 BC, as it was carried south by the Israelite community, who left Egypt for Kush (modern Sudan) during the Judean Rebellion against the Ptolemys in 200 BC. This means it predates the Hasmonean redaction and contains the term Lord (Κύριοσ) instead of Iaô (Ιαω), which, if correctly translated from the Aramaic source texts, would have read ådny (𐤀𐤃𐤍𐤉). The Greeks are believed to have transliterated Yahw (𐤉𐤄𐤅), the Aramaic version of the name Yehvah/Yehvah, as Iaô (Ιαω) in the Book of Leviticus, published circa 250 BC, as evidenced by the Dead Sea Scroll Septuagint fragment 4QpapLXXLev^b, which dates from Hasmonean era Judea. 4QpapLXXLev^b could be interpreted as a Hasmonean redaction of the Septuagint, however, Leviticus appears to have been written during the rule of King Josiah, and his

God was Yahw, supporting the existence of Yahw in the Book of Leviticus.

The Aramaic sections of Masoretic Daniel that were not translated into Hebrew maintain the term adonai ha'elohim (אֲדֹנָי הָאֱלֹהִים), meaning the 'Lord the gods' where the Septuagint has 'Lord the god' (Κύριον τὸν θεὸν), however, the Hebrew sections have Yahweh elohim (יְהוָה אֱלֹהִים) where the Septuagint has 'Lord the god,' suggesting the Greek more accurately reflects the Aramaic source texts than the Hebrew translation. According to some records from the time, this was to repair the damage King Manasseh had done 600 years earlier when he removed the name Yahweh from the Israelite Texts, however, no evidence has survived from the era of Manasseh or earlier that proves the name was originally in the text, suggesting it was an attempt by the first Hasmonean High-Priest/King Simon the Zealot to create a national Judean religion with a god having a name similar to the Roman god Jove.

In the 3rd century AD, the Christians redacted the Septuagint removing the name Iaô, both in Greek, and in Latin translations which transliterated Ιαω as Iaw, replacing it with 'Lord.' This resolved the debate with the Gnostics about whether Iaw was the devil or not. Before that, the various versions of the early Christian-era Septuagint books that included the name, either used Ιαω, or the name written in Hebrew or Phoenician (Paleo-Hebrew) scripts. According to Origen of Alexandria in the late 2nd century AD, the Phoenician (most ancient script) was the most accurate.

According to Theodoret of Cyprus in the 5th century, the Samaritans, who never switched to the Assyrian block letter 'Hebrew,' pronounced the name as Iabe (Ιαβε) or Iabae (Ιαβαι). Hebrews substitute the word 'hasheim,' meaning 'the name,' in all non-scriptural contexts since the Hasmoneans banned the pronunciation of the names of God. Christians have traditionally translated several ways including Jehovah, Jehova, and Jova.

As the original Greek translation of Joshua does not appear to have included the name, the term Lord is used in this translation.

2 Codex Vaticanus: c̄s o t̄h̄s (ⲔⲤⲞⲐⲤ) . Translation: Lord the god

- Aleppo Codex: Yhwh ålhyk (**יהוה אלהיך**). Translation: Yhwh your god

- Leningrad Codex: Yehvah eloheicha (יְהֹוָה אֱלֹהֶיךָ). Translation: Yehwah your god

- Targum Jerusalem: daYeyah elahachon (דַיְיָ אֱלָהֲכוֹן). Translation: the Yahw your god

This verse does not survive in the Dead Sea Scrolls, however, a similar term does show up in later verses that have survived.

- Dead Sea Scroll 4QJosh[a]: Yhwh ålhy (יהוה אלהי). Translations: Yhwh my god

CHAPTER 1 NOTES

The Septuagint's version of the Joshua was translated before 200 BC, as it was carried south by the Israelite community, who left Egypt for Kush (modern Sudan) during the Judean Rebellion against the Ptolemys in 200 BC. This means it predates the Hasmonean redaction and contains the term Lord (Κύριοσ) instead of Iaô (Ιαω), which, if correctly translated from the Aramaic source texts, would have read ådny (אֲדֹנָי). The Greeks are believed to have transliterated Yahw (יְהֹה), the Aramaic version of the name Yehvah/Yehvah, as Iaô (Ιαω) in the Book of Leviticus, published circa 250 BC, as evidenced by the Dead Sea Scroll Septuagint fragment 4QpapLXXLev[b], which dates from Hasmonean era Judea. 4QpapLXXLev[b] could be interpreted as a Hasmonean redaction of the Septuagint, however, Leviticus appears to have been written during the rule of King Josiah, and his God was Yahw, supporting the existence of Yahw in the Book of Leviticus.

The Aramaic sections of Masoretic Daniel that were not translated into Hebrew maintain the term adonai ha'elohim (אֲדֹנָי' הָאֱלֹהִים), meaning the 'Lord the gods' where the Septuagint has 'Lord the god' (Κύριον τὸν θεὸν), however, the Hebrew sections have Yahweh elohim (יְהוָה אֱלֹהִים) where the Septuagint has 'Lord the god,' suggesting the Greek more accurately reflects the Aramaic source texts than the Hebrew translation. According to some records from the time, this was to repair the damage King Manasseh had done 600 years earlier when he removed the name Yahweh from the Israelite Texts, however, no evidence has survived from the era of Manasseh or earlier that proves the name was originally in the text, suggesting it was an attempt by the first Hasmonean High-Priest/King Simon the Zealot to create a national Judean religion with a god having a name similar to the Roman god Jove.

In later copies of the Septuagint, the name was replaced by the name written in Phoenician (𐤉𐤄𐤅𐤄) or Hebrew script (יהוה). The name Iaw is found in fragments of the 3rd century AD Papyrus Oxyrhynchus 1007, however, is represented by a double Yod (יי), meaning it was copied from a later Hebrew or Aramaic text from that era. After the sixth century AD, the occasional copy of the Septuagint is found which uses the name, either written as Ιαω or a Greek approximation of יהוה (ΠΙΠΙ), however, all of these can be traced back to the Hexapla, Quinta, Sextus, and/or Septima, which attempted to retranslate and harmonize the Old Testament in the 3rd through 6th centuries AD. There are no early surviving copies of the Septuagint's version of Joshua which have the name Iaw (Ιαω / 𐤉𐤄𐤅) in it like some of the other books of the Septuagint. As Κυριοσ ο θεοσ translates directly as Lord God (or Lord the God), that term is used.

Chapter 2

Joshua the son of Nun, sent two young men from Shittim[1] to spy on the land, ordering, "Go up, and view the land around Jericho."

The two young men went to Jericho, and entered into the house of a prostitute, whose name was Rehob, and lodged there. It was reported to the king of Jericho, "Men of the sons of Israel have come in here to spy the land."

The king of Jericho sent and spoke to Rehob, ordering, "Bring out the men that entered into your house tonight, as they have come to spy on the land."

The woman took the two men and hid them, and replied to the messengers, "The men came into me, but after the gate was shut in the dark, the men left. I don't know where they've gone. Chase after them, and you may catch them."

She had taken them up onto the roof to the house, and hidden them in flax-stalks that were spread on her on the roof. The left and men chased after them along the road to ford on the Jordan, where the gate was shut. After the men pursuing them had left, and before the spies had gone to sleep, she went up to them on the top of the house, and said, "I know that the Lord has given you the land, as the fear of you, has fallen on us. For we have heard that Lord the god dried up the Papyrus Sea[2] before you, when you came out of the land of Egypt, and all that he did to the two kings of the Amorites, who were beyond Jordan, to Sihon and Og, whom you completely destroyed. When we heard it we were amazed in our heart, and there was no longer any spirit in any of us because of you, for Lord the god is the god in the sky above and on the land below. Now swear to me by Lord the god, since I dealt mercifully with you, you will also deal mercifully with the house of my father, and save the house of my father, my mother, and my brothers, and all my house, and all that they have, and you will rescue my mind from Mot.[3]

The men answered her, "Our life for yours even to death."

She confirmed, "When the Lord has delivered the city to you, you will deal mercifully and truly with me."

She let them down out her window, and she said to them, "Go into the hill-country, in case the pursuers find you, and hide there for three days until your pursuers return from looking for you, and afterward you can leave on your way."

The men said to her, "This is our oath. Look, we will enter into a part of the city, and you will set the sign: you will bind this scarlet cord in the window, by which you have let us down, and you will bring into your house with yourself, your father, and your mother, and your brothers, and all the family of your father. It will come to pass that whoever will be outside the door of your house, his guilt will be on him, and we will be free of this, your oath. We will be responsible for all that will be found with you in your house. But if anyone should injure us, or betray these our matters, we will be free of this, your oath."

She said to them, "Let it be as you have said," and she sent them out, and they departed. They came to the hill-country and remained there for three days, and the pursuers searched all the roads and did not find them. The two young men returned and came down out of the mountain, and they went over to Joshua the son of Nun, and told him all things that had happened to them. They said to Joshua, "The Lord has delivered all the land into our power, and all the inhabitants of that land tremble because of us."

Chapter 2 Notes

1 Codex Vaticanus: Sattin (ϲλττιΝ)

- Aleppo Codex: Štym (שׂטים)

- Leningrad Codex: Shittim (שִּׁטִּ֑ים)

- Targum Jerusalem: Shitin (שִׁטִּין)

The location of the Shittim Valley is generally accepted as Khirbet el-Kafrayn, in Jordan. Other Israelite texts, such as Micah refer to the Lord of Peor in association with the Shittim Valley, however, this name appears to have been an insult directed towards Lord Hammon who was worshiped at Tell el-Hammam in the 800s BC. There is no clear link between Hammon and Peor, implying the worshipers of Peor disappeared around the time the Israelites traveled through the Shittim Valley.

The major ruins in the Shittim Valley, are found at Tell el-Hammam, which was occupied from at least 3600 BC until the beginning of the Late Bronze Age (1550 to 1200) when the site was abandoned for unknown reasons. It was rebuilt in the 900s BC as a Samaritan city. As Tell el-Hammam is in the Shittim Valley, and was destroyed or abandoned when the Israelites moved through the region, using either the traditional Christian dating or the Minoan Eruption and collapse of the Hyksos Dynasty from the Book of Exodus, the Bronze-Age city was likely Peor (Φαγωρ). The exact dating of the abandonment of the bronze-age city is unclear, and there is some evidence of occupation for a few decades after

46

1550 BC, but the site does appear to have been abandoned by 1500 BC.

2 Codex Vaticanus: erythran thalassan (ƐΡΥΘΡΛΝ ѲΛΛΛϹϹΛΝ). Translation: Erythrean (or Red) Sea

• Aleppo Codex: ym swp (יַם סוּף). Translation: sea of reeds (or papyrus)

• Leningrad Codex: yam-suf (יַם־סוּף). Translation: sea of reeds (or papyrus)

• Targum Jerusalem: yama deSuf (יְמָא דְסוּף). Translation: sea of reeds (or papyrus)

The Greek term is not geographically specific, as it is a translation of the Persian term Erostras, which referred to the entire Persian Gulf, Red Sea, and the Indian Ocean. The Greeks were likely referring to the Gulf of Suez, however, this was known to the ancient Egyptians as the 'Sea of Calm,' which is what the Israelites would have called it if that was where they were. The original Sea of Reeds was almost certainly Lake Bardawil on the north coast of the Sinai Peninsula, a shallow saline lake with a surface area of 147,000 acres (59,500 hectares).

The Greeks transliterated the name as the Sea of Siph (ѲΛΛΛϹϹΗϹ ϲιφ) in the Codex Vaticanus' translation of Judges, confirming that the name Swf was in the Aramaic text they worked from. Both the Aramaic term swf (סוּף) and Phoenician term swf (𐤎𐤅𐤐), both meaning papyrus plants were adopted from the Egyptian term tjufi (𓆰𓏤𓈖), which referred to papyrus, papyrus plants, and papyrus marshes. The Egyptian term continued to be used into the Classical era as the Coptic words čoouf (ϫⲟⲟⲩϥ), conf (ϭⲟⲛϥ), and comf (ϭⲟⲙϥ), all meaning papyrus. Conversely, the Egyptian name of the Red Sea was the Sea of Heh (𓇉), meaning 'very large sea' from the Middle Kingdom era onward, however, it is believed to have originally been named after the ancient Egyptian frog god Heh (𓁷).

As the Greek translation of Erythrean Sea is anachronistic, the translation of Papyrus Sea is imported from the Masoretic Text. Based on the described journey out of Egypt, the original Papyrus Sea would have been Lake Bardawil on the north coast of the Sinai Peninsula, a shallow saline lake with a surface area of 147,000 acres (59,500 hectares).

3 Codex Vaticanus: Thanatou (ΘΑΝΑΤΟΥ). Translation: Thanatos (or death, corpse)

• Aleppo Codex: Mwt (מות). Translation: Mot (or 'to die' in Aramaic, 'death' in Hebrew)

• Leningrad Codex: Mavet (מָוֶת). Translation: Mot (or 'death' in Hebrew)

Mot (𐤌𐤕 / ‏‏𐤕𐤌) was the Canaanite god of death, which the Greeks interpreted as the local version of Thanatos, the Greek god of death. The Israelites viewed Mot as the angel of Death in the era of the prophets, which resulted in Thanatos becoming the Christian angel of death in the early centuries of the Christian era.

Chapter 3

Joshua rose early in the morning and left Shittim, and they came as far as the Jordan and lodged there before they crossed over. After three days, the scribes went through the camp, and they ordered the people, "When you see the box[1] of the covenant of Lord the god, and our priests and the Levites carrying it, you will leave from your places, and you will follow it, but keep a distance from it. You will stand at least two thousand cubits from it. Do not approach it, that you may know which way you are to go, as you have not gone this way previously."

Joshua said to the people, "Sanctify yourselves against tomorrow, for tomorrow the Lord will do wonders among you." Joshua said to the priests, "Take up the box of the covenant of the Lord, and go before the people."

The priests picked up the box of the covenant of the Lord and went before the people. The Lord said to Joshua, "Today I begin to exalt you before all the Israelites, that they may know that as I was with Moses, so will I also be with you. Now order the priests that carry the box of the covenant, 'As soon as you enter on a part of the water of Jordan, then you will stand in the Jordan.'"

Joshua said to the Israelites, "Come here and listen to the word of Lord the god. By this you will know that the living God is among you, and will completely destroy from before us the Canaanites, Cypriots,[2] Perizzites, Mitanni,[3] Amorites, Girgashites, and Jebusites. Look, the box of the covenant of the Lord crosses the Jordan. Choose among yourselves twelve men of the sons of Israel, one from each tribe. It will come to pass, when the feet of the priests that carry the box of the covenant of the Lord enter into the water of the Jordan, the water of Jordan below will stop, and the water coming down from above will stop."

The people packed up their tents to cross the Jordan, and the priests carried the box of the covenant of the Lord before the people. When the priests that carried the box of the covenant of the Lord entered on Jordan, and the feet of the priests that carried the box of the covenant of the Lord were stepped into the water of the Jordan, (now the Jordan, its whole channel overflowed all its banks as in the days of the wheat harvest.) Then the waters that came down from above stopped, frozen and exceedingly violent, as far off as the region of Kariathiarim, and that which came down to the Dead Sea (the salt sea),[4] until it completely failed, and the people stood opposite Jericho. The priests that carried the box of the covenant of the Lord stood on dry land in the middle of Jordan, and all the Israelites went through on dry land until all the people had completely crossed the Jordan.

Chapter 3 Notes

1 Codex Vaticanus: cibôton (ΚΙΒШΤΟΝ). Translation: box (or chest)

- Aleppo Codex: årwn (אָרוֹן). Translation: box

- Leningrad Codex: aron (אֲרוֹן). Translation: box

- Targum Jerusalem: aron (אֲרוֹן). Translation: box

The Greek term cibôton (κιβωτὸν) was based on the Aramaic word tybwtå (מ^עֹרוֹטְנָא), however, the Hebrew translation uses a different word, also meaning 'box.' The reason for the Hebrew substitution is likely due to the Aramaic word being based on the Egyptian word djebåt (𓍑𓏤𓈎), meaning 'sarcophagus,' since the classical era, which has resulted in many strange translations. The Egyptian word is accepted as being adopted into Canaanite during the New Kingdom Era, when it was pronounced as debåt (𓂝𓏤𓈎), indicating that the Egyptian word was likely the original in the text. By the Classical era, when the Hebrew text was translated, the related Coptic Egyptian word taibe (ΤΑΙΒЄ) had come to mean coffin, meaning the 'box of god' would have become the 'coffin of god' explaining the Hebrew substitution of årwn (אָרוֹן).

2 Codex Vaticanus: Chettaeon (ΧΕΤΤΑΙΟΝ)

- Aleppo Codex: Ḥty (חתי). Translation: Cypriots

- Leningrad Codex: Chitti (חִתִּי). Translation: Cypriots

- Targum Jerusalem: Chitta'ei (חִתָּאֵי). Translation: Cypriots

This term has created a great deal of confusion since the misidentification of the ruins of the Neshites as being 'Hittite' in the 1800s. The modern archaeological name 'Hittite,' is not derived from an ancient name for the culture applied by themselves, or anyone else, but rather adopted from the biblical reference to a then-unknown civilization somewhere in the region. There was an ancient culture in the region called the Hattians, however, they were conquered by the Nesites before 1700 BC, and subsequently disappeared from the historic records.

The name was applied to culture today referred to as 'Hittites,' before the 'Hittite' language had been translated, and is incorrect. Since 1906, excavations at Boğazköy, the ancient 'Hittite' capital Hattusa have uncovered more than 10,000 'Hittite' texts, including the royal achieve. The actual name of the 'Hittite' language and people was Nešili (𒉈𒅆𒇷), which is now rendered in some academic literate as Nesite or Neshite. As early as the mid-1800s some scholars disputed the identification of the Nesites as the Biblical Hittites, including the Orientalist Max Müller, who was one of many claiming the Biblical Hittites were ancient Greeks or some other Mediterranean people. Later in the Septuagint's translation of the Maccabees, the similar term Chettiim (Χεττιιμ) as a reference to all Greek-speaking lands, and therefore the Biblical Hittites were likely the Minoans or the Achaean Greeks. In the 1st century AD, the Jewish historian Josephus reported that Cethima was the name of Cyrus in Aramaic, and the Chettim were the descendants of Noah's grandson Chethimus, who had settled on Cyprus.

Josephus reported that the name was preserved in the Greek name of the town Cition (Κίτιον). Most historians view it as more likely that the Aramaic name was derived from the city-state of Cition, which was known as Kåtjåy (𓈎𓐍𓏏𓇌𓈙) in Egyptian records from the New Kingdom Era in the late Bronze Age, and Kt (𐤊𐤕) or Kty (𐤊𐤕𐤉) in Phoenician records from the early Iron Age. While this may be the origin of the term, by the era of the Neo-Assyrian era, the term must have also referred to other Greek islands, as both the prophets Isaiah and Ezekiel used the term 'Islands of Kittim.' As the term referred to the entire island of Cyprus in Aramaic, the translations of 'Cyprus' and 'Cypriots' are used here.

3 Codex Vaticanus: Euaion (ΕΥΑΙΟΝ)

- Aleppo Codex: Ḥwy (חוי)

- Leningrad Codex: Chivvi (חִוִּי)

- Targum Jerusalem: Chiva'ei (חִוָּאֵי)

The term is believed to have been derived from the name of the Hurrians, however, is derived separately from the other term Chori (חֹרִי). Chori is accepted as referring to the Hurrians, which the Egyptians called Hårw (𓉔𓄿𓂋𓅱), and the Babylonians called Ḫuurri (𒄯𒊑𒄿). The Hurrians were one of the oldest cultures in the Middle East, however, became largely a slave culture within the Akkadian and Old Babylonian empires. Under the Mitanni empire, they rose to a position of wealth, and formed the noble caste. The Greek transliteration of this term was variations of Chorrhaeous

(Χορραιους), which, like the Hebrew term, was used interchangeably in the texts with Eyaeon (Ευαῖον) / Chivvi (חִוִּי), although that term generally applied to the rules and priests.

The ultimate origin of the terms Eyaeon (Ευαῖον) and Chivvi (חִוִּי), both appear to be the cuneiform word Éan (𒂍𒀭), meaning temple or sacred. In the Amarna Letters, which date to the 1330s BC, the term Éan (𒂍𒀭) was the name of a people, who appear to be the Mitanni, or the Mitanni-Aryan priesthood within the Mitanni. A similar correlation between the terms is found in the Septuagint's 1st Paralipomenon and Masoretic Divrei-hay Yamim, where the Greek translation uses Beithani (Βαιθανι), however, the Hebrew uses the term Mitni (מִתְנִי). This term also refers to a group of people, meaning the underlying Edomite text the Greeks translated would have been 'people of the House of Ån' (𐤉𐤀+𐤕𐤁), a direct Canaanite translation of É An (𒂍𒀭).

While Mitni was the transliteration used in the Edomite text that formed the basis of the Hebrew translation of Divrei-hayYamim, it was replaced with Chivvi (חִוִּי) in the Judahite texts, which served as the basis of most of the Masoretic texts. This likely originated in a Judahite copy of the text, after the Aramaic translation had been made, where an n (𐤍) was replaced with a w (𐤅). The Aramaic translation would have already been made in the time of King Manasseh, were the term was transliterated as Hyån (𐤉𐤀^𐤄𐤕), itself a transliteration of the early Canaanite Ḥyån (𐤉𐤀+𐤆𐤀).

4 Codex Vaticanus: thalassan Araba thalassan alos
(ⲐⲀⲖⲀⲤⲤⲀⲚⲀⲢⲀⲂⲀⲐⲀⲖⲀⲤⲤⲀⲚⲀⲖⲞⲤ). Translation: Sea
of Arabah Sea of Salt

- Aleppo Codex: ym hôrbh ym ḥmlh (**יס הערבה יס המלח**).
Translation: Sea of the Plain sea of salt

- Leningrad Codex: yam ha'aravah yam-hammelach (יָם
הָעֲרָבָה יָם־הַמֶּלַח). Translation: Sea of the Plain sea of salt

- Targum Jerusalem: leyama demeishra leyama demilcha
(לְיַמָּא דְמֵישְׁרָא לְיַמָּא דְמִלְחָא). Translation: the sea of the valley
the sea of salt

The Sea of Arabah was an ancient name for the Dead Sea.
The scribal notes clarifying that the Sea of Arabah was the salt
sea appears to have been included in the Aramaic source text
that both the Septuagint and Masoretic versions of Joshua
were translated from. The fact that the Aramaic translator
needed to clarify which sea the Sea of Arabah was, suggests
the Aramaic translation of Joshua was made in the north,
likely in Gilead or Aram. This note also means the original
Book of Joshua was not written in Aramaic, but translated
from another language, and, clearly written earlier, when
the term Sea of Arabah was commonly used.

Chapter 4

When the people had completely crossed the Jordan, the Lord said to Joshua, "Take men from the people, one from each tribe, and organize them, and you will take out of the middle of the Jordan twelve existing stones, and having carried them across together with yourselves, place them in your camp, where you will camp for the night."

Joshua called twelve distinguished men among the Israelites, one of each tribe, and said to them, "Advance before me in the presence of the Lord into the middle of Jordan, and each pick up a stone from there, let him carry it on your shoulders, according to the number of the twelve tribes of Israel. These may be for you continually an appointed sign, so when your son asks you in the future, 'What are these stones to us?' Then you may explain to your son, 'The river Jordan was dried up from before the box of the covenant of the Lord when it passed it, and these stones will be as a memorial for you for the Israelites forever."

The Israelites did so, as the Lord commanded Joshua. They picked up twelve stones out of the middle of Jordan, (as the Lord commanded Joshua when the Israelites had completely crossed over,) and carried these stones with them into the camp, and laid them down there. Joshua set also another twelve stones in Jordan itself, in the place that was under the feet of the priests that carried the box of the covenant of the Lord, and there they are to this day. The priests that carried the box of the covenant stood in Jordan until Joshua had finished all that the Lord commanded him to report to the people, and the people rushed and crossed over. When all the people had passed over, that the box of the covenant of the Lord crossed over, and the stones before them. The sons of Reuben, and the sons of Gad, and the half-tribe of Manasseh crossed equipped before the Israelites, as Moses commanded them. Forty thousand armed for battle went over before the Lord to war, to the city of Jericho. On that day the Lord magnified Joshua before all the people of Israel, and they were afraid of him, like they had been of Moses, as long as he lived.

The Lord said to Joshua, "Order the priests that carry the box of the covenant of the testimony of the Lord, to come up out of Jordan."

Joshua ordered the priests, "Come up out of Jordan."

When the priests who carried the box of the covenant of the Lord had come up out of Jordan and set their feet on the land, the water of the Jordan returned rapidly to its place and went as before over all its banks. The people came out of the Jordan on the tenth day of the first month, and the Israelites camped at the circle[1] in the region eastward from Jericho. Joshua set these twelve stones which he took out of Jordan, in a circle, and said, "When your sons ask you, 'What are these stones? Tell your sons, that Israel came over the Jordan on dry land when Lord the god had dried up the water of Jordan from before them until they had passed over. As Lord the god did to the Papyrus Sea, which Lord the god dried up from before us until we passed over. That all the nations of the earth might know, that the power of the Lord is mighty and that you might worship Lord the god in every work."

Chapter 4 Notes

1 Codex Vaticanus: Galgaloes (ΓΑΛΓΑΛΟΙC)

- Aleppo Codex: glgl (גלגל). Translation: circle

- Leningrad Codex: gilgal (גִּלְגָּל). Translation: circle

- Targum Jerusalem: gilgala (גִּלְגָּלָא). Translation: wheel

Gilgal (גִּלְגָּל) is the Hebrew word for circle. Archaeologists have discovered several ceremonial stone circles in Canaan that were used between 1200 and 1000 BC for gatherings that are assumed to be religious in nature. As these stone circles are found down in the valleys, unlike the altars at the tops of hills where the Canaanites worshiped, and 'circles' (גלגל) are mentioned throughout the old Israelite texts, it is assumed they are early Israelite religious centers from before the First Temple was built.

Chapter 5

When the kings of the Amorites who were beyond Jordan heard, and the kings of Phoenicia[1] by the sea, that Lord the god had dried up the river Jordan from before the Israelites when they passed over, that their hearts failed, and their minds melted, and there was no sense in them in the face of the Israelites.

About this time the Lord said to Joshua, "Make yourself stone knives from sharp stone, and sit down and circumcise the Israelites the second time."

Joshua made sharp knives of stone, and circumcised the Israelites at the place called the 'Hill of Foreskins.' This is how Joshua purified the Israelites, as many as were born in the way, and as many as were uncircumcised of them that came out of Egypt, all these Joshua circumcised. For forty-two years Israel wandered among the abandoned places of desert-dwellers.[2] Therefore most of the fighting men that came out of the land of Egypt were uncircumcised, those who disobeyed the commands of God, concerning who he determined should not see the land, which the Lord swore to give to their fathers, a land flowing with milk and honey.

In their place he raised up their sons, who Joshua circumcised, because they were uncircumcised, having been born long the way. When they had been circumcised they rested sitting there in the camp until they were healed.

The lord[3] said to Joshua the son of Nun, "On this day have I removed the reproach of Egypt from you," and he called the name of that place Gilgal.

The Israelites kept the Passover on the fourteenth day of the month in the evening, to the west of Jericho on the opposite side of the Jordan in the plain. They ate the grain of the earth unleavened and new grain. On this day the manna stopped after they had eaten of the grain of the land, and the Israelites no longer had manna. They took the fruits of the land of the Phoenicians in that year. When Joshua was in Jericho, that he looked up with his eyes and saw a man standing before him, and there was a drawn sword in his hand, and Joshua approached and said to him, "Are you with us, or on the side of our enemies?"

He answered him, "I have now come, the Generalissimo of the army of the Lord."[4]

Joshua fell on his face to the earth, and said to him, "Lord, what do you command of your servant?"

The Generalissimo of the Lord said to Joshua, "Remove your shoes off your feet, for the place on which you now stand is sacred."

Chapter 5 Notes

1 Codex Vaticanus: Phoenicês (ϕΟΙΝΙΚΗϹ). Translation: Phoenicia

- Aleppo Codex: Knôny (כנעני). Translation: Canaan

- Leningrad Codex: Kena'ani (כְּנַעֲנִי). Translation: Canaan

- Targum Jerusalem: Chena'ana'ah (כְּנַעֲנָאָה). Translation: Canaan

Phoenicia and Canaan were two names of the same land and culture. Phoenicia is believed to be derived from the Egyptian name of the people, which then sped through the Mediterranean. Canaan is believed to be derived from the Akkadian name for the people, which was mainly used in Semitic languages of the Middle East. Both terms are believed to be derived from the name 'purple people,' as the Canaanites were mass exporters of purple dye and fabric throughout most of their civilization.

2 Codex Vaticanus: tê erêmô tê Madbaritidi (ΤΗΕΡΗΜѠ ΤΗΜΑΔΒΑΡΙΤΙΔΙ). Translation: the desert the Madbarites

- Aleppo Codex: mdbr (מדבר). Translation: the desert

- Leningrad Codex: midbar (מִדְבָּר). Translation: the desert

- Targum Jerusalem: madbera (מַדְבְּרָא). Translation: the desert

The Greek translation deviates from the Hebrew and Judeo-Aramaic translations, which simply refer to the desert. The

Greek could either be read as the 'desert of the Madbarites,' or the 'abandoned places of the Madbarites.' The term Madbaritidi (Μαδβαριτιδι) is a synthesis of the Aramaic mdbrå (ܐܪܒܕܡ) meaning 'desert' and the Greek -itidi (-ιτιδι), meaning 'people of,' the precursor to the modern English '-ites.' This means the term had to be adopted from a term in the Aramaic text which translates as 'desert dweller.' Based on the context, the Aramaic word was likely mdbråyn (ܢܝܐܪܒܕܡ), meaning 'desert-dweller.' This means the Aramaic text either read the redundant 'desert of the desert-dwellers,' or 'abandoned places of the desert-dwellers,' which is the interpretation used in this translation. As desert-dwellers are nomadic, is suggested the Israelites had occupied their settlements while they were elsewhere.

3 Codex Vaticanus: c̄s̄ (ΚϹ). Translation: lord

- Aleppo Codex: Yhwh (יהוה)

- Leningrad Codex: Yehvah (יְהֹוָה)

- Targum Jerusalem: Yeyah (??). Translation: Yahw

Based on the requirement to re-institute the Egyptian practice of circumcision, in order to remove the 'reproach of Egypt,' this appears to be describing the Israelites rejoining Egyptian civilization, which would make the 'lord' in the text King Thutmose I, before the Hasmoneans carelessly changed him to Yahweh.

4 Codex Vaticanus: architstratêgos dynameôs c̄u̅ (ΑΡΧΙϹΤΡΑΤΗΓΟϹ ΔΥΝΑΜΕШϹ K̄Y̅). Translation: Generalissimo (or high strategist, supreme commander) of the forces of the Lord

- Aleppo Codex: šr ṣbå yhwh (שַׂר צְבָא יהוה). Translation: minister of the army of Yhwh

- Leningrad Codex: sar-tzeva-Yehvah (שַׂר־צְבָא־יְהוָה). Translation: minister of the army of Yehwah

- Targum Jerusalem: Mal'ach sheliach min kodam Yeyah (מַלְאַךְ שְׁלִיחַ מִן קֳדָם יְיָ). Translation: messenger-agent from before Yahw

While the Greeks gave the 'Generalissimo' an impressive rank, the Masoretic texts simply call him a minister or secretary, and the later Jerusalem Targum labels him as a messenger-agent. Assuming that this was not a reference to a supernatural being, or some extraterrestrial being, it was likely the commander of the Egyptian army who was campaigning in Canaan in the year this story is set according to the Septuagint's chronology. Jericho was destroyed, its walls pulled down around the time that the Egyptian army passed through the region, and most Egyptologists accept that the Egyptian army destroyed the city, regardless of whatever the Israelites were doing there.

Chapter 6

Now Jericho was closely sealed up and besieged, and none went out of it, and none came in.

The Lord said to Joshua, "Look, I deliver Jericho into your power, and its king in it, and its mighty men. Set the warriors around it. It will be that when you will sound with the trumpet, all the people will shout together. When they have shouted, the walls of the city will fall by themselves, and all the people will enter, each one rushing directly into the city."

Joshua the son of Nun went to the priests, and said to them, "Let seven priests having seven sacred trumpets proceed before the Lord, and let them sound loud, and let the box of the covenant of the Lord follow. Order the people to go round, and circle the city, and let your warriors pass by armed before the Lord. Let the warriors proceed before, and the priests bringing up the rear behind the box of the covenant of the Lord proceed sounding the trumpets."

Joshua commanded the people, saying, don't cry out, nor let anyone hear your voice until he himself declares to you the day to cry out, and then you will cry out. The box of the covenant of God having gone around immediately returned into the camp and lodged there. On the second day Joshua rose in the morning, and the priests picked up the box of the covenant of the Lord. The seven priests bearing the seven trumpets went on before the Lord, and afterward, the warriors went on, and the remainder of the multitude went after the box of the covenant of the Lord, and the priests sounded with the trumpets. All the rest of the multitude circled the city six times from within a short distance and went back again into the camp. They did this for six days.

On the seventh day, they rose early and circled the city on that day seven times. It happened at the seventh circuit the priests blew the trumpets, and Joshua said to the Israelites, "Shout, for the Lord has given you the city. The city will be cursed and, and all things that are in it, to Lord Sabaoth,[1] only save Rehob the prostitute, and all things in her house. But keep yourselves strictly from the cursed things, in case you change your mind and take the cursed things, and you make the camp of the Israelites a cursed thing and destroy us. All the silver, or gold, or brass, or iron, will be holy to the Lord. It will be carried into the treasury of the Lord."

The priests sounded with the trumpets, and when the people heard the trumpets, all the people shouted at once with a loud and strong shout, and all the walls fell around it, and all the people went up into the city. Joshua devoted it to destruction and all things that were in the city, man and woman, young man and old, and calf and donkey, by the edge of the sword.[2]

Joshua said to the two young men who had acted as spies, "Go into the house of the woman, and bring her out here, she and all that she has."

The two young men who had spied out the city entered into the house of the woman, and brought out Rehob the prostitute, and her father, and her mother, and her brothers, and her families, and all that she had, and they took her out to the camp of Israel. The city was burnt with fire with all things that were in it, only the silver, and gold, and brass, and iron, they brought into the treasury of the Lord. Joshua saved Rehob the prostitute, and all the house of her father, and allowed her to live in Israel until this day because she hid the spies which Joshua sent to spy out Jericho. Joshua adjured them on that day before The Lord, saying, "Cursed be the man who will build that city, he will lay the foundation of it in his firstborn, and he will set up the gates of it in his youngest son."

(As did Hozan of the Temple of El. He laid the foundation with Abiram, his firstborn, and set up the gates of it with his youngest surviving son.)

The Lord was with Joshua, and his name was in all the land.

Chapter 6 Notes

1 Codex Vaticanus: Cyriô Sabaôth (ΚΥΡΙѠ ϹΑΒΑѠΘ). Translation: Lord Sabaoth (or 'forces' in Hebrew, 'desires' in Aramaic)

- Aleppo Codex: Yhwh (יהוה). Translation: Yhwh

- Leningrad Codex: Yehvah (יְהֶוָה). Translation: Yehwah

- Targum Jerusalem: Yeyah (יְּי). Translation: Yahw

This reference to Lord Sabaoth is clearly earlier than the Hasmonean redaction, which replaced most referenced to the various Lords of Canaan with Yhwh. In this case, the entire term Lord Sabaoth was replaced by Yahweh in the Hasmonean redaction, indicating that they considered Lord Sabaoth to be a proper name, and not a title. According to Greek and Roman records from the era, as well as the books of Maccabees, the Judahites worshiped Lord Sabaoth during the Greek rule of Judea. The Greeks associated Lord Sabaoth with Dionysus, while the Romans associated Lord Sabaoth with Bacchus.

Immediately after the Maccabean Revolt had successfully driven out the Greeks and established the Hasmonean Dynasty, the Judeans sent an emissary to Rome to request an alliance against the Greeks, but Roman records indicate that the result was all Judeans being evicted from Rome because the Judean emissaries claimed that their god 'Jupiter Sabazious' was the Roman god Jupiter. As this was the earliest Roman records of a Judean god with a name like Jupiter's (Latin: Iuppiter or Iovis), it seems the first

70

Hasmonean King/High-Priest Simon the Zealot was responsible for the resurgence of the name Yhwh, which completely replaced Lord Sabaoth before the end of the Hasmonean dynasty.

2 The walled city of Jericho, which has been identified as Tell es-Sultan since 1869, was destroyed sometime circa 1500 BC, and the site was virtually unoccupied until after 1000 BC. The site has been studied extensively, with various dates given for its destruction ranging from 1700 to 1400 BC. The cause of the collapse of the walls is unknown, however, it is theorized, depending on when the walls fell, that they may have been ripped down by the Egyptians circa 1500 BC, as Thutmose I's army campaigned all the way to the Euphrates, however, according to Thutmose I's records, they found no one to fight in Canaan, implying someone had recently campaigned in the region. He claimed that the Canaanite chieftains had pledged loyalty to Egypt, however, archaeological evidence shows after 1500 BC fortifications began being built throughout Canaan.

Chapter 7

But the Israelites committed a great crime and plundered some of the cursed things. Achan the son of Carmi, the son of Zabdi, the son of Zerah, of the tribe of Judah, took of the cursed things, and the Lord was very angry with the Israelites. Joshua sent men to the government office, which is by the Temple of El, ordering, "Spy out the government office,"[1] and the men went up and spied on Gai.

They returned to Joshua, and reported to him, "Don't send all the people up, but send about two or three thousand men up to capture the city by siege. Don't send up there all the people, as the enemy are few."

About three thousand men when up, and they fled from the men of Gai. The men of Gai killed thirty-six of them, and chased them from the gate, and drove them from the steep hill, and the heart of the people was alarmed and became like water. Joshua tore his garments and fell to the earth on his face before the Lord until evening, both he and the elders of Israel, and they threw dirt on their heads.

Joshua said, "I beg, Lord, has your servant brought these people across the Jordan to deliver them to the Amorites to destroy us? We should have remained and settled ourselves beyond Jordan. What will I say since Israel has turned his back before his enemy? When the

CHAPTER 7

Canaanites and all the inhabitants of the land hear it, they will surround us and destroy us from off the land. What will you do for your great name?"

The Lord answered Joshua, "Get up! Why have you fallen on your face? The people have sinned and transgressed the covenant which I made with them. They have stolen cursed things and put them into their store. The Israelites will not be able to stand before their enemies. They will turn their back before their enemies, as they have become a cursed thing! I will no longer be with you unless you remove the cursed thing from yourselves. Rise! Sanctify the people and tell them to sanctify themselves for the morning, so says Lord the god of Israel. The cursed thing is among you. You will not be able to stand before your enemies until you have removed the cursed things from among you. You will all be gathered together by your tribes in the morning, and the tribe which the Lord will indicate, you will bring by families. The family which the Lord will indicate, you will bring by household, and the household which the Lord will indicate, you will bring man by man. The man who will be pointed out will be burnt with fire, and all that he has, because he has transgressed the covenant of the Lord, and has worked wickedness in Israel."

CHAPTER 7

Joshua rose early and brought the people by their tribes, and the tribe of Judah was indicated. It was brought by their families, and the family of the Zerahites was indicated. It was brought man by man, and Achan the son of Zabdi the son of Zerah was indicated. Joshua said to Achan, "Give glory this day to Lord the god of Israel, and make a confession, and tell me what you have done, and don't hide it from me."

Achan answered Joshua, "Indeed I have sinned against Lord the god of Israel. I did this: I saw in the spoil an embroidered mantle, and two hundred shekels[2] of silver, and one golden wedge of fifty shekels, and I wanted them and took them, and look, they are hidden in my tent, and the silver is hidden under them."

Joshua sent messengers, and they ran to the tent in the camp, and these things were hidden in his tent, and the silver under them. They brought them out of the tent and brought them to Joshua and the elders of Israel, and they laid them before the Lord. Joshua took Achan the son of Zerah and brought him to the valley of Achor, and his sons, and his daughters, and his calves, and his donkeys, and all his sheep, and his tent, and all his property, and all the people were with him. He brought them to Emec Achor. Joshua asked Achan, "Why have you destroyed us? The Lord will destroy you today."

CHAPTER 7

All Israel stoned him with stones. They set up over him a great heap of stones, and the Lord ceased from his fierce anger. Therefore he called the place Emecachor until this day.

Chpater 7 Notes

1 Codex Vaticanus: Gai (ܪܐܝ)

- Aleppo Codex: Hôy (הֵעִי)

- Leningrad Codex: Ha'ai (הָעָי)

- Targum Jerusalem: ay (עָי). Translation: ruins

The Greek translators transliterated this word two different ways from the Aramaic texts they translated. In Genesis it was transliterated as Aggai (Αγγαι), however, both the geographic location and the Hebrew translation of Hôy (הֵעִי) confirm it is the same location. The Hebrew term is often translated as 'ruins' however, the place is inhabited during the era of Joshua, indicating 'ruins' is an incorrect interpretation. The term appears to have originated with the Middle Egyptian word Kha (𓉐), meaning 'government office,' and several 'Khas' are mentioned as existing in Canaan. This 'government office' was the one Abram had built an altar near when he first entered Canaan.

As Canaan had been under the control of the Egyptians during the Middle Kingdom era, as well as during the Canaanite and Hyksos dynasties of the Second Intermediate Period, the colonial offices appear to have been continuously occupied. In the year the story is set, 1504 BC, the armies of Thutmose I had just marched through Canaan, however, he does not appear to have reclaimed the old 'government office' in Samaria, and based on the Israelites attacking 'Gai' immediately after removing the 'reproach of Egypt,' by re-instituting the Egyptian custom of circumcision, and attacking

Jericho with the 'Generalissimo of the forces of the Lord,' it suggests that the Israelites attacked the 'government office' for the Egyptians. By the era of Joshua, this Gai appears to have become a town, and the term is used as a proper name.

2 Codex Vaticanus: didrachma (ΔΙΔΡΑΧΜΑ). Translation: two-drachmas

- Aleppo Codex: šqlym (שׁקלים). Translation: shekels

- Leningrad Codex: shekalim (שְׁקָלִים). Translation: shekels

- Targum Jerusalem: sal'in (סַלְעִין). Translation: selas

The shekel was a unit of weight used throughout the Middle East for thousands of years, weighing approximately 8.6 grams of silver. The Greek drachma was a coin weighing approximately half a shekel, and therefore under Greek rule of the Middle East, a two-drachma coin was used. As the Greeks clearly translated shekel into didrachma, the term shekel is restored in this translation. The term sela, used as the Targum Jerusalem, was a similarly sized coin and weight from the late classical era.

Chapter 8

The Lord said to Joshua, "Don't be afraid or nervous. Take with you all the warriors, and rise, and go up to Gai. I have given into your hands the king of Gai and his land. You will do to Gai, as you did to Jericho and its king, and you will take for yourself the spoils of its livestock. Set an ambush behind the city."

Joshua and all the warriors rose to go up to Gai, and Joshua chose out thirty thousand mighty men, and he sent them away by night. He ordered them, "You lie in ambush behind the city, near the city, and you will all remain ready. I and all with me will come close to the city, the inhabitants of Gai will come out to meet us like before, and we will flee from before them. When they will come out after us, we will draw them away from the city. They will say, 'These men flee from before us, like before.' You will rise up out of the ambuscade, and go into the city. You will do according to this word. Look, I have commanded you."

Joshua sent them, and they went to lie in ambush, and they lay between the Temple of El[1]   and the government office, to the west of Gai.

Joshua rose early in the morning and reviewed the people, and he went up, he and the elders before the people to Gai. All the warriors went up with him, and they went forward and approached the city from the east. The ambuscade was on the west side of the city. When the king of Gai saw it, he rushed and went out to meet them immediately in battle, he and all the people that were with him, and he did not know that there was an ambuscade positioned against him behind the city. Joshua and Israel saw them and retreated from before them, and they chased after the Israelites, and traveled a distance from the city. There was no one left in Gai who did not chase after Israel, and they left the city open when they chased after Israel.

The Lord said to Joshua, "Stretch out your hand with the spear towards the city, for I have delivered it into your hands, and those laying in wait will rise quickly from their place."

Joshua stretched out his hand and his spear towards the city, and the ambuscade rose quickly out of their place, and entered into the city and captured it. They quickly set the city on fire. When the inhabitants of Gai looked around them, then they saw the smoke going up out of the city to the sky, and they were no longer able to flee this way or that way. Joshua and all Israel saw that the ambuscade had taken the city and that the smoke of the city went up to the sky, and they turned and attacked the men of Gai. These came out out of the city to meet them, and they were in the middle of the army, some being on this side, and some on that, and they slaughtered them until there was none left of them who survived and escaped.

They took the king of Gai alive and brought him to Joshua. When the Israelites had finished slaying all that were in Gai, and in the fields, and in the mountain on the descent, from where they pursued them even to the end, then Joshua returned to Gai and struck it with the edge of the sword. They who died on that day, men and women were twelve thousand, all the inhabitants of Gai. Beside the spoils that were in the city, all things which the Israelites took as spoil for themselves according to the command of the Lord, as the Lord commanded Joshua. Joshua burnt the city with fire, he made it an uninhabited heap forever, even to this day.

He hanged the king of Gai on a doubletree, and he remained on the tree until evening. When the sun went down, Joshua gave the order, and they took down his body from the tree and threw it into a trench, and they set over him a heap of stones until this day.

Chapters 8 Notes

1 Codex Vaticanus: Baethêl (ΒΛΙΘΗΛ)

- Aleppo Codex: byt ål (בית אל). Translation: house (or temple) of El (or god)

- Leningrad Codex: veit-el (בֵית־אֵל). Translation: house (or temple) of El (or god)

- Targum Jerusalem: beit el (בֵית אֵל). Translation: house (or temple) of El (or god)

The term Bethel meant several things in ancient Canaan. The term translates as 'house of god,' which can be translated as either 'Temple of God (or El)' or 'sky/heaven.' Bethel was worshiped as a god by the ancient Canaanites, the brother of El and Dagon according to Sanchuniathon, who referred to him as Baitylos, which is the name used in this translation when the god is denoted. The term can also be translated as 'meteorite' as meteorites were believed to be parts of the god Baitylos that had fallen to the Earth, and shrines were built around them. A Temple of El was built in the region by Jacob in Genesis and appears to have been a major town by the time of Joshua.

Chapter 9

When the kings of the Amorites on the other side of Jordan, who were in the mountain country, and in the plain, and in all the coast of the great sea, and those who were near Anti-Lebanon, and the Cypriots, Canaanites, Perizzite, Mitanni, Amorites, Girgashites, and Jebusites heard, they came in an alliance to make war against Joshua and Israel.

Then Joshua built an altar to Lord the god of Israel on Mount Ebal, as Moses the servant of the Lord commanded the Israelites, as it is written in the law of Moses, an altar of uncarved stones, against which iron had not been lifted. There he offered whole burnt offerings to the Lord and a peace offering. Joshua wrote on the stones a copy of the law of Moses, before the Israelites. All Israel, and their elders, and their judges, and their scribes passed on one side and on the other before the box. The priests and the Levites took up the box of the covenant of the Lord. The foreigners and the natives were there, who were half of them near Mount Gerizim and half near Mount Ebal, as Moses the servant of the Lord commanded at first, to bless the people.

Afterward, Joshua read accordingly all the words of this law, the blessings, and the curses, according to all things written in the law of Moses. There was not a word of all that Moses ordered Joshua, which Joshua read not in the ears of all the assembly of the Israelites, the men, and the women, and the children, and the strangers that joined themselves to Israel.

The inhabitants of Gibeon heard of all that the Lord did to Jericho and Gai. They worked cunningly, and they went and made provisions and prepared themselves, and having taken old sacks on their shoulders, and old and tore and patched bottles of wine, and the upper part of their shoes and their sandals old and clouted on their feet, and their old garments on them, and the bread in their provisions was dry, moldy, and partially eaten.

They came to Joshua at the camp of Israel at the circle, and said to Joshua and Israel, "We have come from a far off land, now then make a covenant with us."

The Israelites replied to the Hurrians,[1] "Suppose you live among us, how should I make a covenant with you?"

They replied to Joshua, "We are your servants."

Joshua asked them, "Where are you from, and where have you come from?"

They answered, "Your servants have come from a very far country in the name of Lord the god, for we have heard his name, and all that he did in Egypt, and all that he did to the kings of the Amorites, who were

CHAPTER 9

beyond Jordan, to Sihon king of the Amorites, and Og king of Bashan, who lived in Ashteroth and in Edrei. Our elders and all that inhabit our land when they heard said to us, 'Take with yourselves provision for the journey and go to meet them, and you will say to them, 'We are your servants, and now make a covenant with us.' These are the loaves we took hot for our journey on the day on which we came out to come to you, and now they are dried and have become moldy. These are the skins of wine which we filled when new, and they are torn, and our garments and our shoes are worn out because of the very long journey."

The chiefs took of their provision and asked no counsel of the Lord. Joshua made peace with them, and they made a covenant with them to protect them, and the princes of the congregation swore to them. Three days after they had made the covenant with them, they heard that they were near neighbors and that they lived among them. The Israelites departed and came to their cities, and their cities were Gibeon, and Kefireh,[2] and Beirut,[3] and the cities of Ye'arim,[4] and the Israelites did not fight with them, because all the princes swore to them by Lord the god of Israel, and all the congregation murmured at the princes.

The princes said to all the congregation "We have sworn to them by Lord the god of Israel, and now we will not be able to touch them. We will do this, we will capture them alive, and we will preserve them, so there will be no anger against us, because of the oath which we swore to them. They will live and will be lumber-jacks and drawers of water for all the congregation," as the princes swore to them.

Joshua called them together and asked them, "Why have you deceived me, saying, 'We live very far from you, whereas you are fellow-countrymen of those who live among us? Now you are cursed. There will not be any of you that is not a slave, or a lumberjack, or a drawer of water for me and my god."

They answered Joshua, "It was reported to us that Lord the god ordered his servant, Moses, to give you this land, and to destroy us and all that lived on it before you. We were very afraid for our lives because of you, and therefore we did this thing. Now look, we are in your power. Do to us as it is pleasing to you, and as it seems good to you."

They did so to them, and Joshua rescued them on that day out of the hands of the Israelites, and they did not kill them. Joshua made them on that day lumberjacks and drawers of water to the whole congregation, and for the altar of God. Therefore the inhabitants of Gibeon became lumberjacks and drawers of water for the altar of

God until this day, even for the place which the Lord should choose. Then Joshua built an altar to Lord the god of Israel on Mount Ebal, as Moses the servant of the Lord commanded the Israelites, as it was written in the law of Moses, an altar of uncarved stones, on which iron had not been lifted, and he offered there whole burnt offerings to the Lord, and a piece offering. Joshua wrote on the stones a copy of the law of Moses, before the Israelites. All Israel, and their elders, and their judges, and their scribes passed on one side and on the other, before the box, and the priests, the Levites took up the box of the covenant of the Lord. The stranger and the native were there, who were half of those near Mount Ebal, as Moses the servant of the Lord commanded before, to bless the people.

Chapter 9 Notes

1 Codex Vaticanus: Chorrhaeon (ϰΟΡΡΑΙΟΝ). This is a Greek transliteration of Chori (חֹרִי), the term generally believed to refer to the Hurrians.

- Aleppo Codex: Ḥwy (חוי)

- Leningrad Codex: Chivvi (חִוִּי)

- Targum Jerusalem: Chiva'ah (חִוָאָה)

There were two terms used in the Septuagint and Masoretic Text for the Hurrians: Chorrhaeon / Chori (Χορραῖον / חֹרִי) and Euaion / Chivvi (Εὐαῖον / חִוִּי), however, in this case, the names do not match between the Septuagint and Masoretic Text, indicating that there were two versions of Joshua in circulation. The terms are both believed to derive from the same culture, however, are not interchangeable.

The name Chorrhaeon / Chori, often transliterated as Horite, referred to the Hurrian people, while the term Euaion / Chivvi, referred to the Mitanni-Aryan nobility or Vedic priests. This difference between the Greek and Hebrew texts cannot be accounted for through a transliteration error, or the assumption that the Greeks decided to use the same term for both people, as Euaion (Εὐαῖον) was already used in the Book of Joshua. Hurrians are documented in southern Canaan at the time, as the Adbi-Heba, the chieftain of Jerusalem, had a Hurrian name in the Amarna Letters, circa 1335 BC.

2 Codex Vaticanus: Cephira (ΚΕΦΙΡΑ)

- Aleppo Codex: Kpyrh (כפירה)
- Leningrad Codex: Kefirah (כְּפִירָה)
- Targum Jerusalem: Chefirah (כְפִירָה)

This is believed to be Khirbet Kefireh in the West Bank of Palestinian Territories.

3 Codex Vaticanus: Bêrôth (ΒΗΓΩΘ)

- Aleppo Codex: Bårwt (בארות)
- Leningrad Codex: Ve'erot (בְּאֵרוֹת)
- Targum Jerusalem: Ve'erot (בְּאֵרוֹת)

The location of this town is disputed. Some sources claim it is Al-Bireh, while others claim it is Biddu, both in the West Bank of Palestinian Territories. The Hebrew name is identical to the Phoenician name of Beirut, Bårt (𐤁𐤓𐤕), however, the modern Hebrew spelling of Beirut is Byyrwt (ביירות), derived from the Arabic Bayrūt (بيروت).

The term used in the Septuagint is not the Greek name for Beirut, which is Bêrytos (Βηρυτός), however, all sources agree that the terms found in the Masoretic Text and Septuagint are variant spellings of Beirut, although the town in question is believed to have been in the West Bank, and not Lebanon.

4 Codex Vaticanus: Iarin (ιѧριℵ)

- Aleppo Codex: Qryt Yôrym (**קרית יערים**)

- Leningrad Codex: Qiryat Ye'arim (קִרְיַ֖ת יְעָרִים)

- Targum Jerusalem: Qiryat Ye'arim (קִרְיַת יְעָרִים)

The location of this town is generally assumed to be at the same location as the modern town of Kiryat Ye'arim in Israel.

Chapter 10

When King Adonibezec[1] of Jerusalem heard that Joshua had taken Gai and had destroyed it. That as he'd done to Jericho and its king, he had also done to Gai and its king, and that the inhabitants of Gibeon had gone over to Joshua and Israel, then they were greatly terrified by them, for the king knew that Gibeon was a great city, one of the mother cities, and all its men were mighty. So King Adoni-bezek of Jerusalem sent messages to King Hoham of Hebron, and King Piram of Jarmuth, and King Japhia of Lachish, and King Debir of Adullam, saying, "Come up here to me, and help me, and let us take Gibeon, because the Gibeonites have gone over to Joshua and to the Israelites."

The five kings of the Jebusites went up, the king of Jerusalem, and the king of Hebron, and the king of Jarmuth, and the king of Lachish, and the king of Adullam, they and all their people, and camped around Gibeon, and besieged it. The inhabitants of Gibeon sent word to Joshua at the camp by the circle, saying, "Do not delay from your servants. Come up quickly to us, and help us and save us. All the kings of the Amorites who live in the hill country are gathered against us."

Joshua went up from the circle, he and all the warriors with him, everyone mighty in strength. The Lord said to Joshua, "Don't fear them, for I have delivered them into your hands. There will not be one of them left."

When Joshua came suddenly on them, he had advanced all night from the circle. The Lord struck them with terror before the Israelites, and the Lord destroyed them in a great slaughter at Gibeon, and they chased them by the road going up to the House of Horon,[2] and they slaughtered them to Azekah and to Makkedah. When they fled from the face of the Israelites at the descent of Temple of Horon, then the Lord threw hailstones on them from the sky to Azekah, and more died by the hailstones, than those who the Israelites killed with the sword in the battle.

Then Joshua spoke to the Lord, in the day in which the Lord delivered the Amorites into the power of Israel when he destroyed them in Gibeon, and they were destroyed from before the Israelites. Joshua said, "Let the sun stand over Gibeon and the moon over the valley of Ayalon."

The sun and the moon stood still until God executed vengeance on their enemies, and the sun stood still in the middle of the sky. It did not proceed to set until the end of one day. There was not a day like it either before or after, that god should listen to man because the Lord fought on the side of Israel. The five kings fled, and hid in a cave in Makkedah.

Joshua was told, "The five kings have been found hidden in the cave in Makkedah." Joshua said, "Roll stones to the mouth of the cave and set men to watch over them. Don't stand still, but chase after your enemies and seize of them, and do not allow them to enter into their cities, for Lord the god has delivered them into our hands."

When Joshua and all Israel stopped slaughtering them, they that escaped took refuge in the fortified cities. All the people returned healthy to Joshua at Makkedah, and none of the Israelites murmured with his tongue. Joshua said, "Open the cave, and bring out these five kings from the cave."

They brought the five kings out of the cave, the king of Jerusalem, and the king of Hebron, and the king of Jarmuth, and the king of Lachish, and the king of Adullamite. When they brought them out to Joshua, he called together all Israel, and the chiefs of the army that went with him, and said to them, "Come forward and set your feet on their necks," and they came and set their feet on their necks.

Joshua said to them, "Do not fear them or be cowardly. Be courageous and strong, as the Lord will do this to all your enemies against who you fight."

Joshua killed them and hanged them on five trees, and they hung on the trees until the evening. Towards the setting of the sun, Joshua commanded, and they took them down from the trees and threw them into the cave which they had fled for refuge, and they rolled stones into the cave, which remain until this day. They took Makkedah on that day and killed the inhabitants with the edge of the sword, and they completely destroyed every living thing that was in it, and there was none left in it that was preserved and had escaped. They did to the king of Makkedah, as they did to the king of Jericho. Joshua and all Israel with him departed out of Makkedah to Libnah and besieged Libnah. The Lord delivered it into the hands of Israel, and they took it and its king and killed the inhabitants with the edge of the sword, and everything breathing in it. Nothing was left in it that survived and escaped, and they did to its king as they did to the king of Jericho. Joshua and all Israel with him departed from Libnah to Lachish, and he camped around it and besieged it.

The Lord delivered Lachish into the hands of Israel, and they took it on the second day, and they put the inhabitants to death with the edge of the sword, and completely destroyed it, as they had done to Libnah. Then Horam the king of Gezer went up to help Lachish, and Joshua slaughtered him and his people with the edge of the sword until there was none left of him that was safe and escaped. Joshua and all Israel with him departed from Lachish to Adullam, and he besieged it and attacked it. The Lord delivered it into the hand of Israel, and he took it on that day, and killed the inhabitants with the edge of the sword, and killed everything breathing in it, as they did to Lachish.

Joshua and all Israel with him departed to Hebron and camped around it. He struck it with the edge of the sword, and all the living creatures that were in it. There was no one left alive. They destroyed it and all things in it, as they did to Adullam. Joshua and all Israel returned to Debir, and they camped around it, and they took it, and its king, and its villages. He struck it with the edge of the sword, and they destroyed it, and everything breathing in it. They did not leave in it anyone alive.

They did to Hebron and her king, as they did to Debir and her king. Joshua struck all the land of the hill country, and Negev and the plain country, and Azzah, and her kings, they did not leave of them one alive. They completely destroyed everything that had the breath of life, as Lord the god of Israel commanded, from Kadesh Barnea[3] to Gaza, all Goshen, as far as Gibeon.

CHAPTER 10

Joshua slaughtered, once for all, all their kings, and their land, because Lord the god of Israel fought on the side of Israel.

Chapter 10 Notes

1 Codex Vaticanus: Adônibezec (ᴀᴅⲱⲛⁱᴮᴇᴢᴇⲕ)

- Aleppo Codex: ådny Sdq (אדני צדק). Translation: Lord Sydyk (or of Justice)

- Leningrad Codex: Adoni-Tzedek (אֲדֹנִי־צֶ֖דֶק). Translation: Lord Sydyk (or of Justice)

- Targum Jerusalem: Adoni Tzedek (אֲדֹנִי צֶדֶק). Translation: Lord Sydyk (or of Justice)

The Greek translators treated the term as a name, Adônibezec, however, the Hebrew translation treats it as a title 'Lord of Justice.' The two translations also deviate on whether it was bezec (βεζεκ) or zedek (צֶ֖דֶק), which cannot simply be a transliteration error, as the Greeks knew of the Canaanite god Sydyk, and transliterated his name as Sydyc (Συδυκ). Adônibezec is a transliteration of a Semitic term, meaning essentially the 'My Lord in Strength' in Canaanite and Aramaic. During the Roman era, Sydyk was viewed as the Canaanite version of Jupiter, the supreme God of the Roman Empire. As the Septuagint does not agree with the Masoretic Text, the Greek name is used in this translation.

2 Codex Vaticanus: Ôrônin (ⲱⲣⲱⲛⁱⲛ)

- Aleppo Codex: byt Hwrn (בית חורן). Translation: House (or Temple) of Horon

- Leningrad Codex: veit-Chovron (בֵית־חֹורֹ֔ן). Translation: House (or Temple) of Horon

• Targum Jerusalem: veit Choron (בֵּית חוֹרוֹן). Translation: House (or Temple) of Horon

Horon was one of the Canaanite underworld gods. He was one of the sons of Mot (Death), who himself later became the Israelite messenger of death Mot, and early Christian angel of death Thanatos. Hwårn (𓀀𓏏𓆓𓄿𓈗) was also a god of death in ancient Egypt, and the source of the Greek psychopomp Charon (Χάρων) according to Diodorus Siculus. The town around the Temple of Horon is also listed in the inscriptions at the Temple of Karnak, in Egypt, as 'Batae Houarn' in Egyptian hieroglyphs, one of the towns that Pharaoh Sheshonq I attacked, circa 925 BC, which was later recorded in the 3ʳᵈ Kingdoms (Masoretic Kings). During the era of the two kingdoms, the twin towns of Upper and Lower Beth-Horon served as border towns. These towns have been identified as the Palestinian villages of Beit Ur al-Fauqa and Beit Ur al-Tahta, in the West Bank.

3 Codex Vaticanus: Cadês Barnê (ΚΛΔΗϹΒΑΡΝΗ)

• Aleppo Codex: qdš brnô (קדש ברנע). Translation: Sacred Barnea

• Leningrad Codex: Kadesh Barnea' (קָדֵשׁ בַּרְנֵעַ). Translation: Sacred Barnea

• Targum Jerusalem: Rekam gei'ah (רְקָם גֵּיאָה). Translation: Petra (or stony, rocky) hills

The location of Kadesh Barnea has been debated since the Second Temple Era. The Jewish general and historian Josephus reported that the sacred books salvaged from the Second Temple when it was destroyed by the Romans placed Kadesh Barnea at Petra, in modern Jordan. He also claimed that Mount Sinai was nearby, which is the source of the claim that Mountain of the Altar (Jebel al-Madhbah) was Mount Sinai. The name Kadesh Barnea is undoubtedly named after an ancient deity, as the first word, Kadesh (קָדֵשׁ), means holy or sacred. The name Barnea is presumably the name of the deity in question, and the general Hebrew pronunciation of the name as Varne'a is quite similar to the name Mitannian god Aruna, the equivalent of the Vedic god Varuna.

As Deuteronomy chapter 2 reports that Hurrians were living in Seir before the Edomites killed them and inhabited the region, this would support the name Aruna being the source of Barnea, as the Hurrians were the major population base of the Mitanni Empire. This connection between the Mitannian Indo-Aryan Varuna worshipers at Mount Seir would also explain how Mitra-Varuna (𐎹𐎠𐎼 𐎭𐎾𐎡) entered into Judaism, as his earliest recorded Hebrew name Mttrwn (מטטרון) is essentially the same as the Mitannian god of covenants Miitra-Aruna, and played the same role in the Vedic Texts as Metatron did in Second Temple Era Judaism. Subsequent Hebrew pronunciations of the name from the Medieval Era, Mttrwn (מטטרון), Metateron (מֶטָטְרוֹן), Metatron (מְטַטְרוֹן), Meitatron (מֵיטַטְרוֹן), Mitatron (מִיטַטְרוֹן), and Mattatron (מַטַטְרוֹן), as well as the Arabic Mītatrūn

(ميططرون), are all influenced by the Greek pronunciation of the name Metà-thrónos (Μετὰ-θρόνος), which means 'next to the throne.'

Chapter 11

When King Jabin of Hazor heard, he sent word to King Jobab of Madon, and to the king of Shimron, and the king of Achshaph, and the kings who were by the Sidon the Great,[1] to the hill country and to Arabah across Chinneroth, and to the plain, and to Phenaeddor, and to the Canaanites on the coast to the east, and to the Amorites on the coast, and the Cypriots, and the Perizzites, and the Jebusites in the mountain, and the Mitanni, and those living at the foot of Mount Hermon in the land of Mizpeh. They went out with their kings, like the sand of the sea in numbers, with horses, and a great many chariots. All the kings assembled in person, and came to the same place, and camped at the waters of Madon to make war with Israel.

The Lord said to Joshua, "Do not be afraid of them, for tomorrow at this time I will make them run from Israel. You will hamstring their horses, and burn their chariots with fire."

Joshua and all the warriors suddenly attacked them at the water of Madon and followed them into the hill country. The Lord delivered them into the power of Israel, and they struck them and chased them to Sidon the Great,[2] and to Maseron,[3] and to the plains of Mizpeh in the east. They destroyed them until there was not one of them left that survived. Joshua did to them, as the

Lord commanded him, he mutilated their horses, and burnt their chariots with fire.

Joshua returned after that and took Hazor and her king. Previously Hazor was the chief of these kingdoms. They killed with the sword all that breathed in it and completely destroyed them all, and there was nothing living left in it. They burnt Hazor with fire. Joshua took all the cities of the kingdoms, and their kings, and killed them with the edge of the sword, and completely killed them, as Moses the servant of the Lord commanded.

But Israel did not burn all the walled cities, only Hazor was burnt. The Israelites took all its spoils for themselves, and they killed all the men with the edge of the sword, until they destroyed them, and they left none of them breathing. As the Lord commanded his servant Moses, Moses also commanded Joshua, and this Joshua did, he transgressed no law of all that Moses commanded him. Joshua took all the hill country, and all the land of Negev, and all the land of Goshen, and the plain country, and that towards the west, and the mountain of Israel and the low country by the mountain, from the mountain of Halak, and that which goes up to Seir, and as far as Ba'al Gad,[4] and the plains of Lebanon under Mount Hermon.

CHAPTER 11

He took all their kings and destroyed and killed them. For many days, Joshua waged war with these kings. There was no city which Israel did not capture. They took it all in war. For the Lord had hardened their hearts to go out to war against Israel, so they might be completely destroyed, and mercy should not be granted to them, but that they should be completely destroyed, as the Lord told Moses.

Joshua came at that time, and completely destroyed the Anaks[5] out of the hill country, from Hebron and from Debir, and from Anab, and from all the race of Israel, and from all the mountain of Judah with their cities, and Joshua completely destroyed them. There was not anyone left of the Anaks near the Israelites, there were only some of them in Gaza, and in Gath, and in Ashdod. Joshua took all the land, as the Lord commanded Moses, and Joshua gave it for an inheritance to Israel by division according to their tribes, and the land war ended.

Chapter 11 Notes

1 Codex Vaticanus: Sidôna tên megalên (ϹΙΔШΝΔΤΗΝ ΜΕΓΔΛΗΝ). Translation: Sidon the great

• Aleppo Codex: Spwn bhr (צפון בהר). Translation: Zephon (or north) on mountain

• Leningrad Codex: Tzefovn bahar (צָפֹון בָּהָר). Translation: Zephon (or north) on mountain

• Targum Jerusalem: Tzepuna betura (צְפוּנָא בְּטוּרָא). Translation: Zephon at mountain

The Greek and Hebrew translations differ at this point. The reference to Sidon as the great city, found in the Greek at this point, and also the Hebrew and Aramaic Targums later in the chapter, would date the original text to earlier than circa 980 BC, when Sidon was the mother city of the Phoenicians. Between 980 and 947 BC, King Hiram of Tyre, led the Tyrians in challenging the dominance of Sidon. The Hebrew translation of Mount Zephon (צפון בהר) instead of Sidon is unlikely to have been a Hasmonean redaction, and is something that was likely retained in the Judahite (or Samaritan) texts that the Hebrew translators worked from. Mount Zephon was the holy mountain of northern Canaan, where the temple of the storm-god Ba'al Hadad was located.

2 Codex Vaticanus: Sidônos tês megalês (ϹΙΔШΝΟϹΤΗϹ ΜΕΓΔΛΗϹ). Translation: Sidon the great

• Aleppo Codex: Sydwn rbh (צידון רבה). Translation: great Sidon

- Leningrad Codex: Tzidovn Rabbah (צִידוֹן רַבָּה).
Translation: great Sidon

- Targum Jerusalem: Tzidovn rabbeta (צִידוֹן רַבְּתָא).
Translation: great Sidon

3 Codex Vaticanus: Maserôn (ΜΑϹΕΡѠΝ)

- Aleppo Codex: mšrpwt mym (**משרפות מים**). Translation:
crematoria waters

- Leningrad Codex: misrefovt mayim (מִשְׂרְפוֹת מַיִם).
Translation: crematoria waters

- Targum Jerusalem: chartzei yama (חַרְצֵי יַמָּא). Translation:
sharps (or sharp things, cutting things, cuts) seas

This is considered an unknown location at the southern
border of Sidonian control on the Mediterranean coast. It is
most likely a reference to the glass production facilities of
Sidon, which were the city's largest export during the Late-
Bronze Age. As this trade disappeared in the early Iron Age,
it would place the origin of the Book of Joshua before the
Bronze Age Collapse.

4 Codex Vaticanus: Baalgad (ΒΑΑΛΓΑΔ)

- Aleppo Codex: Bôl Gd (**בעל גד**)

- Leningrad Codex: Ba'al Gad (בַּעַל גָּד)

• Targum Jerusalem: shar Gad (שַׂר גָד). Translation: prince (or commander) Gad

Ba'al Gad was an ancient Canaanite god, the god of luck, and the god that Jacob's son Gad was named after, and therefore the entire tribe of Gad.

5 Codex Vaticanus: Enacim (ΕΝΑΚΙΜ)

• Aleppo Codex: Ônqym (עֲנָקִים). Translation: giant, huge, large, big, neck, necklace, Anaks (an ancient tribe of Canaan)

• Leningrad Codex: Anakim (עֲנָקִים). Translation: giant, huge, large, big, neck, necklace, Anaks (an ancient tribe of Canaan)

• Targum Jerusalem: gibbaraya (גִבָּרַיָא). Translation: strong men (or giants, heroes)

The Anaks were transliterated as Enach (Εναχ) in the Book of Numbers, but translated as Gigantes (Γιγάντων) in the Book of Deuteronomy, implying the Greeks considered the Anaks to be like the Gigantes of ancient Greece, who fought a war against the Olympian gods, and lost. The Anaks were a tribe of people also referred to in the book of Judges. According to the book of Judges, they apparently lived in Hebron. The Egyptian Execration Texts from the Middle Kingdom record a group of Canaanites called the 'Anaq' who are generally considered to be the same people.

Chapter 12

These are the kings of the land, whom the Israelites killed, and inherited their land beyond Jordan from the east, from the valley of Arnon to Mount Hermon, and all the land of Arabah on the east. Sihon king of the Amorites, who lived in Heshbon, ruling from Arnon, which is in the valley, on the slope of the valley, and half of Gilead as far as Jabbok, the borders of the Ammonites. Arabah as far as the sea of Galilee[1] to the east, and as far as the Dead Sea, the salt sea to the east by the way to Asimoth, from Teman under Azzah Phasga. King Og of Bashan, who lived in Ashteroth and in Edrei, was what remained of the Gigantes[2] ruling from Mount Hermon and from Salcah, and over all the land of Bashan to the borders of Gergesi, and Machi and the half of Gilead of the borders of Sihon king of Heshbon. Moses the servant of the Lord and the Israelites struck them down, and Moses gave them by way of inheritance to Reuben, and Gad, and to the half-tribe of Manasseh.

These are the kings of the Amorites, who Joshua and the Israelites killed beyond Jordan by the sea of Ba'al Gad in the plain of Lebanon, and as far as the mountain of Halak, as men go up to Seir, and Joshua gave it to the tribes of Israel to inherit according to their portion, in the mountain, and in the plain, and in Arabah, and in Azzah, and in the wilderness, and the Negev, the Cypriots, Amorites, Canaanites, Perizzites, Mitanni, and Jebusites.

CHAPTER 12

The king of Jericho, and the king of Gai, which is near the Temple of El, the king of Jerusalem, the king of Hebron, the king of Jarmuth, the king of Lachish, the king of Eglon, the king of Gezer, the king of Debir, the king of Geder, the king of Hormah, the king of Arad, the king of Libnah, the king of Adullam, the king of Elath, the king of Tappuah, the king of Hepher, the king of Aphek of Aroc, the king of Hushim, the king of Shimron, the king of Mambroth, the king of Achshaph, the king of Kadesh, the king of Zachac, the king of Maredoth, the king of Jecom of Carmel, the king of Adullam belonging to Phennealdor, the king of Gei of Galilee, and the king of Tirzah. All these were twenty-nine kings.

Chapter 12 Notes

1 Codex Vaticanus: Chenereth (ⲭⲉⲛⲉⲣⲉⲟ)

- Aleppo Codex: Knrwt (כנרות)

- Leningrad Codex: Kinarot (כִּנֲרוֹת)

- Targum Jerusalem: Ginosar (גִּינוֹסַר)

These are all alternate names for the region around the Sea of Galilee, also known as Lake Tiberius.

2 Codex Vaticanus: gigantôn (ⲅⲓⲅⲁⲛⲧⲱⲛ). Translation: Gigantes

- Aleppo Codex: Rpåym (ורפאיס). Translation: long-dead (in Canaanite), giants (modern Hebrew), Rephaites (theoretical ancient tribe)

- Leningrad Codex: Refa'im (רְפָאִים). Translation: long-dead (in Canaanite), giants (modern Hebrew), Rephaites (theoretical ancient tribe)

- Targum Jerusalem: gibbaraya (גִבָּרַיָא). Translation: strong men (or giants, heroes)

The Rpåm (𐤉𐤀𐤓𐤐) were a semi-deified long-dead people by the 1200s BC, as the Ugaritic Texts include the so-called Rephaim Text. They appear to be an ancient people that had been deified and were believed to live in the underworld. The word's etymology implies they were healers. The fact that they were described as 'ruling from Mount Hermon' implies they were the 'watchers' from the Enochian tradition.

The similarities between the name Enach / Ônq (Εναχ / עֲנָק) and Enôch / Ḥnwk (Ενωχ / חֲנוּךְ) may have led to the confusion in the translation, resulting in both Ônqym (עֲנָקִים) and Rpåym (רְפָאִים) as Gigantes in different places in the books of Numbers, Deuteronomy, and Joshua. As the Books of Enoch had to have been translated also before the Beta Israel community left Egypt during the rebellion of 200 BC, the Books of Enoch must have been translated at the same time, and likely by the same translators.

Chapter 13

When Joshua was old and advanced in years, the Lord said to Joshua, "You are advanced in days, and there is much land left to inherit. This is the land that remains: the borders of the Pelesets,[1] the Geshurites, and the Canaanite, from the wilderness near Egypt, as far as the borders of Ekron on the left of the Canaanites the land is reckoned to the five principalities of the Pelesets, to the inhabitants of Gaza, Ashdod, Ashkelon, Gath, and Ekron, and to the Mitanni from Teman, to all the land of Canaan before Gaza, and the Sidonians as far as Aphek, as far as the borders of the Amorites."

"All the land of Giblites of the Pelesets, and all Lebanon east of the circle, under Mount Hermon as far as the entering in of Hamath, everyone that inhabits the hill country from Lebanon as far as Masereth Memphomaim. All the Sidonians, I will destroy them from before Israel, but you give them by inheritance to Israel, as I ordered you. Now divide this land by lot to the nine tribes, and to the half-tribe of Manasseh. From Jordan to the Mediterranean Sea in the west, you will give it to them. The Mediterranean Sea will be the boundary."

"But to the two tribes and to the half-tribe of Manasseh, to Reuben and to Gad Moses gave an inheritance beyond Jordan, Moses the servant of the Lord gave it to them eastward, from Aroer, which is on the bank of the brook of Arnon, and the city in the middle of the valley, and all Misor from Medeba. All the cities of Sihon king of the Amorites, who reigned from Heshbon to the borders of the Ammonites, and the region of Gilead, and the borders of the Geshurites and the Maachathites, the whole of Mount Hermon, and all the land of Bashan to Acha. All the kingdom of Og in the region of Bashan, who reigned in Ashteroth and in Edrei, he was left of the Raphites, and Moses killed him and destroyed him."

But the Israelites did not destroy the Geshurites and the Maachathites and the Canaanites, and the king of the Geshurites and the Maachathites lived among the Israelites until this day. Only no inheritance was given to the tribe of Levi, Lord the god of Israel is their inheritance, as the Lord told them. This is the division that Moses made to the Israelites in Araboth Moab, on the other side of Jordan, by Jericho. Moses gave the land to the tribe of Reuben according to their families. Their borders were from Aroer, which is opposite the brook of Arnon, and theirs is the city that is in the valley of Arnon; and all Misor, to Heshbon, and all the cities in Misor, and Debir, and Bamoth-Ba'al, and the house of Baal-Meon, and Bashan, and Bakedmoth, and Maephaad, and Kariathaim, and Shibmah, and Serada, and Sior on Mount Emak,[2] and the House of Peor,[3] and Azzah

Phasga, and the House of Jeshimoth, and all the cities of Misor, and all the kingdom of Sihon king of the Amorites, who Moses killed, both he and the princes of Midian,[4] Evi,[5] Petra,[6] Zur,[7] and Hur,[8] and Prince Reba of the remnants of Sihon, and the inhabitants of the land.

Balaam the son of Beor the prophet they killed in the battle. The borders of Reuben were at the Jordan, which was the boundary. This is the inheritance of the children of Reuben according to their families, these were their cities and their villages. Moses gave an inheritance to the sons of Gad according to their families. Their borders were Jazer, all the cities of Gilead, and half the land of the Ammonites to Arabah, which is before Arad. From Heshbon to Araboth by Massepha, and Betonim, and Mahanaim to the borders of Debir, and Enadom, and Othargai, and the House of Nimrah, and Succoth, and Zaphon, and the rest of the kingdom of Sihon king of Heshbon, and Jordan will be the boundary as far as part of the Sea of Galilee,[9] beyond Jordan to the east. This is the inheritance of the children of Gad according to their families and according to their cities. According to their families, they will turn their backs before their enemies, because their cities and their villages were according to their families.

Moses gave to half the tribe of Manasseh according to their families. Their borders were from Mahanaim, and all the kingdom of Bashan, and all the kingdom of Og king of Bashan, and all the villages of Jair, which are in the region of Bashan, sixty cities, and the half of Gilead, and in Ashteroth, and in Edrei, royal cities of Og in the land of Bashan, Moses gave to the sons of Machir the sons of Manasseh, including to the half-tribe sons of Machir the sons of Manasseh, according to their families. These are those who Moses allowed to inherit beyond the Jordan, in Araboth Moab, and beyond Jordan east of Jericho.

Chapter 13 Notes

1 Codex Vaticanus: Phylistiim (ΦΥΛΙϹΤΙΙΜ). Translation: Philistines (or Pelesets, Pelesets)

- Aleppo Codex: Plštym (**פלשתים**). Translation: Philistines (or Palestinians, Pelesets)

- Leningrad Codex: Pelishtim (פְּלִשְׁתִּים). Translation: Philistines (or Palestinians, Pelesets)

- Targum Jerusalem: Pelishta'ei (פְּלִשְׁתָּאֵי). Translation: Philistines (or Palestinians, Pelesets)

The Pelesets were an ancient people based in the region of the modern Gaza Strip of the Palestinian Territories. The earliest surviving mention of them is from the reliefs of the Temple of Ramses III at Medinet Habu in Egypt that dates back to some time between 1186 and 1155 BC, in which they were called Pwråsåtj (𓂋𓏤𓊪𓈙𓏏𓇌), commonly anglicized as Pelesets. They were also known in Middle Babylonian as the ᵏᵘʳPalastu (𒆳𒉺𒆷𒊍𒌅).

It is unclear where they came from, however, one theory is that they were the Pala, a Luwian people from the Black Sea coast of Anatolia. The region was an independent country called Palaa (𒆳𒉺𒆷𒀀) in the Neshite (Hittite) records from the 1600s BC, however, have become part of the Nesite Empire by the 1500s BC. Around the time the Pelesets invaded Canaan, the Pala were driven from their homeland by the neighboring Kaskians from northeast Anatolia, which supports the connection between the groups, however, it has yet to be proven conclusively.

The presence of the Pelesets in Southern Canaan during the time of Joshua is anachronistic, as the Egyptians recorded the Pelesets arriving in the 1200s BC. At the time, the Egyptians recorded that the Hanubu were the dominant population in Sinai, which is believed to have been a reference to the Minoans, however, they disappeared from the region shortly after the Minoan erruption. Therefore this section of text, describing the origin of the Semitic tribes, found in both the Septuagint and the Masoretic text, likely dates to the original Phoenician translation in the early Iron Age, by which time the name Hanubu was no longer recognized.

2 Codex Vaticanus: Emac (ЄΜΛΚ)

• Aleppo Codex: ômq (עמק). Translation: valley (or vale, lowland, open country)

• Leningrad Codex: emek (עֵמֶק). Translation: valley (or vale, lowland, open country)

• Targum Jerusalem: meishra (מֵישְׁרָא). Translation: plain (or valley)

3 Codex Vaticanus: Baethphogôr (ΒΛΙΘΦΟΓѠΡ)

• Aleppo Codex: Byt Pôwr (בית פעור). Translation: House (or Temple) of Pwr

• Leningrad Codex: Veit Pe'ovr (בֵית פְּעֹור). Translation: House (or Temple) of Peor

• Targum Jerusalem: Veit Pe'or (בֵית פְּעוֹר). Translation: House (or Temple) of Peor

This verse has not survived among the Dead Sea Scrolls. There are no known locations associated with the name Peor, which implies the location was abandoned after the events of Joshua. Other Israelite texts, such as Micah refer to the Lord of Peor in association with the Shittim Valley, however, this name appears to have been an insult directed towards Lord Hammon who was worshiped at Tell el-Hammam in the 800s BC.

There is no clear link between Hammon and Peor, implying the worshipers of Peor disappeared around the time the Israelites passed through the Shittim Valley. The major ruins in the Shittim Valley, are found at Tell el-Hammam, which was occupied from at least 3600 BC until the beginning of the Late Bronze Age (1550 to 1200) when the site was abandoned for unknown reasons. It was rebuilt in the 900s BC as a Samaritan city. As Tell el-Hammam is in the Shittim Valley and was destroyed or abandoned when the Israelites moved through the region, using either the traditional Christian dating or the Minoan Eruption and collapse of the Hyksos Dynasty from the Book of Exodus, it is likely that the Bronze-Age city was Peor (Φαγωρ). The exact dating of the abandonment of the bronze-age city is unclear, and there is some evidence of occupation for a few decades after 1550 BC, but the site does appear to have been abandoned around 1500 BC, meaning Joshua would have had to have destroyed it around them.

4 Codex Vaticanus: Madiam (ΜΑΔΙΑΜ). Translation: Midian

- Aleppo Codex: Mdyn (מדין). Translation: Midian

- Leningrad Codex: Midyan (מִדְיָן). Translation: Midian

- Targum Jerusalem: Midyan (מִדְיָן). Translation: plain (or valley)

5 Codex Vaticanus: Eui (ΕΥΙ)

- Aleppo Codex: Åwy (אוי)

- Leningrad Codex: Evi (אֱוִי)

- Targum Jerusalem: Evi (אֱוִי)

6 Codex Vaticanus: Rocom (ΡΟΚΟΜ)

- Aleppo Codex: rqm (רקם). Translation: Petra

- Leningrad Codex: reqem (רֶקֶם). Translation: Petra

- Targum Jerusalem: reqem (רֶקֶם). Translation: Petra

Raqmu was the ancient name of Petra, in modern southwest Jordan. By the era of the kingdoms of Judah and Samaria, the region was known as Sela (סֶלַע), suggesting this section of text is older.

7 Codex Vaticanus: Sour (ϹΟΥΡ)

- Aleppo Codex: Ṣwr (צור). Translation: Zur (or rock)

- Leningrad Codex: Tzur (צוּר). Translation: Zur (or rock)

- Targum Jerusalem: Tzur (צור). Translation: Zur (or rock)

Based on the other locations in southern Canaan, this is probably a reference to Beth-Zur, in the West Bank, south of Jerusalem.

8 Codex Vaticanus: Oyr (ΟΥΡ)

- Aleppo Codex: ḥwr (חור). Translation: white

- Leningrad Codex: chur (חוּר). Translation: white

- Targum Jerusalem: chur (חור). Translation: watch (or look)

This appears to be a reference to Tell es-Safi near Hebron, an ancient fortress from the Bronze Age, built on a hill composed of white cliffs. The site has been occupied continuously since the 5th millenium BC.

9 Codex Vaticanus: thalassês Chenereth (ΘΑΛΑϹϹΗϹ ΧΕΝΕΡΕΘ). Translation: Sea of Chinnereth

- Aleppo Codex: ym Knrt (ים כנרת). Translation: Sea of Chinnereth

- Leningrad Codex: yam-Kinneret (יָם־כִּנֶּרֶת). Translation: Sea of Chinnereth

- Targum Jerusalem: yam Ginosar (יַם גִּינוֹסַר). Translation: sea of Ginosar

These are all alternate names for the Sea of Galilee, also known as Lake Tiberius.

Chapter 14

These are those of the Israelites that received their inheritance in the land of Canaan, to who Eleazar the priest, and Joshua the son of Nun, and the heads of the families of the tribes of the Israelites, gave inheritance. They inherited according to their lots, as the Lord commanded by the hand of Joshua to the nine tribes and the half-tribe, on the other side of Jordan. But to the Levites, he gave no inheritance among them. For the sons of Joseph were two tribes, Manasseh and Ephraim, and there was no inheritance in the land given to the Levites, only cities to live in, and their suburbs separated for the livestock, and their livestock. As the Lord commanded Moses, so the Israelites did when they divided the land.

The children of Judah came to Joshua at the circle, and Caleb the son of Jephunneh the Kenezite said to him, "You know the word that the Lord spoke to Moses the man of God concerning me and you in Kadesh Barnea. For I was forty years old when Moses the servant of God sent me out of Kadesh Barnea to spy out the land, and I returned him an answer according to his mind."

"My brothers that went up with me turned away the heart of the people, but I chose to follow the Lord, my God. Moses swore on that day, 'The land on which you have gone up, it will be your inheritance and your children's forever, because you have chosen to follow Lord the god.' Now the Lord has kept me alive as he said."

"This is the forty-fifth year since the Lord spoke that word to Moses, and Israel journeyed in the wilderness, and now look, I am on this day eighty-five years old. I am still strong this day, like when the Lord sent me. Just as strong am I now to go out and to come in for war. Now I ask of you this mountain, as the Lord said on that day, for you heard this word on that day, and now the Anaks are there, cities great and strong. If then the Lord should be with me, I will completely destroy them, as the Lord told me."

Joshua blessed him and gave Hebron to Caleb the son of Jephunneh the son of Kenez for an inheritance. Therefore Hebron became the inheritance of Caleb the son of Jephunneh the Kenezite until this day because he followed the commandment of Lord the god of Israel. The name of Hebron was previously the city Argob, it was the mother city of the Anaks, and the land rested from war.

Chapter 15

The borders of the tribe of Judah according to their families were from the borders of Edom from the Wilderness of Zin, as far as Kadesh to the south. Their borders were from the south as far as a part of the salt sea from the high country that extends to the south. They follow from the ascent of Akrabbim, and go out around Zenan, and go up from the south to Kadesh Barnea, and go out to Hezron, and proceed up to Adar, and go out by the way that is west of Karkaa. They go out to Zalmonah and start at the valley of Egypt, and the end of its boundaries will be at the sea. These are their boundaries to the south.

Their boundaries to the east are along the salt sea and the Jordan.

The borders in the north are from the seacoast, and part of the Jordan, the borders go up to the House of Hoglah, and continue along the north to the House of Arabah, and up to the stone of Bohan the son of Reuben. The borders continue on to the quarter of the valley of Achor, and go down to the circle which is at the approach to Adummim, which is to the south in the valley, and terminate at the water of the Fountain of Shemesh,[1] and from there go to the Fountain of Rogel. The borders go up to the valley of Hinns,[2] behind Jebus to the south (this is Jerusalem). The borders terminate at the top of the mountain, which is before the valley of Hinns towards the west, (which is next to the land of the Raphites of the north). The border going out from the top of the mountain terminates at the fountain of the water of Nephtoah and terminates at Mount Ephron, and the border will lead to Baalah (this is the city of Jarim).

The border will go around Baalah to the sea and will go on to Mount Seir behind the city of Jearim to the north (this is Chesalon). It will come down to the Temple of Shemesh and will go on to the south. The border terminates behind Ekron to the north, and the borders will terminate at Booths, and the borders will go on to the south and will terminate at Libnah, and the start of the borders will be at the sea. Their borders will be at the sea, the great sea will be the boundary. These are the borders of the children of Judah according to their families.

To Caleb the son of Jephunneh, he gave a portion in the middle of the children of Judah by the command of God. Joshua gave him the city of Arboc the mother-city of Anaks (this is Hebron). Caleb the son of Jephunneh destroyed the three sons of the Anaks there: Susi, and Tholami, and Achima.

Caleb went up there to the inhabitants of Debir. (The name of Debir was previously the City of Letters before.)[3] Caleb offered, "Whoever will take and destroy the City of Letters, and conquer it, to him will I give my daughter Acsah as a wife."

Othniel the son of Kenaz the brother of Caleb took it, and he gave Acsah his daughter to him as a wife. As she left she counseled him, "I will ask of my father a field, and she called from her donkey."

Caleb asked her, "What do you have to say?"

She answered him, "Give me a blessing, as you have set me to the land of Negev. Give me Botthanis."

He gave her Upper Gonaethla, and Lower Gonaethla. This is the inheritance of the tribe of the children of Judah.

The cities belonging to the tribe of the children of Judah on the borders of Edom by the wilderness where: Kabzeel, Ara, Hazor, Icam, Regma, Aruel, Kadesh, Asorionain, Maenam, Balmaenan, and their villages, and the cities of Hezron: Hazor, Sen, Salmaa, Molada, Seri, Bethpalet, Hazarshual, and Beersheba, and their villages, and their hamlets: Baalah, Bacoc, Hushim, Eltolad, the Temple of El, Hormah, Ziklag, Macharim, Sethennac, Lebaoth, Sale, and Eromoth. Twenty-nine cities, and their villages.

CHAPTER 15

In the plain country: Eshtaol, Raa, Assa, Ramen, Tano, Iluthoth, Maeani, Jermuth, Adullam, Membra, Socoh, Jazeca, Sharaim, and Gederah and its villages; fourteen cities and their villages.

Zenan, Hadashah, Migdalgad, Dilean, Mizpeh, Joktheel, Bozkath, Ideadalea, Chabra, Maches, Maachos, Gederoth, Temple of Dagon, Naamah, Makkedah; sixteen cities, and their villages.

Libnah, Ether, Anoch, Jana, Nezib, Keilah, Achzib, Kezib, Bathesar, and Elon; ten cities and their villages.

Ekron and her villages, and their hamlets. From Ekron: Gemna and all the cities that are near Azzah, and their villages.

Asiedoth, and her villages and hamlets.

Gaza, and its villages and hamlets as far as the river of Egypt, and the Mediterranean Sea[4] is the boundary.

In the hill country: Shamir, Jetheth, Socha, Renna, and the City of Letters (this is Debir),[5] and Anon, Es, Anim, Aesam, Goshen, Chalu, Channa, Giloh; eleven cities, and their villages.

Aerem, Remna, Soma, Janum, Bethtappuah, Aphekah, Humtah, and the city Arboc, (this is Hebron) and Zior; Nine cities and their villages.

Maon, Carmel, Ozib, Itan, Jezreel, Aricam, Zacanaim, Gibeah, and Thimnathah; nine cities, and their villages.

Halhul, House of Zur, Gedor, Maarath, the Temple of Anat, Eltekon; six cities, and their villages.

Theco, Ephrath, this is House of Lehem, Phagor, Aetan, Culon, Tatam, Thobes, Carem, Galem, Thether, and Manocho; eleven cities, and their villages.

The Town of Baal (this is the city of Jarim), and Sotheba; two cities and their villages.

Baddargeis, Tharabaam, Aenon, Aeochioza, Naphlazon, and the cities of Sadon, and Ancades, seven cities, and their villages.

The Jebusite lived in Jerusalem, and the children of Judah could not destroy them. (The Jebusites live in Jerusalem to this day.)

Chapter 15 Notes

1 Codex Vaticanus: Êliou (ΗΛΙΟΥ). Translation: Helios (or sun)

- Aleppo Codex: šmš (שמש). Translation: Shemesh (or sun)

- Leningrad Codex: shemesh (שֶׁמֶשׁ). Translation: Shemesh (or sun)

- Targum Jerusalem: shemesh (שְׁמֶשׁ). Translation: Shemesh (or sun)

Shemesh was the Canaanite sun god, whose worship was later banned by King Josiah.

2 Codex Vaticanus: pharanga Onom (ΦΑΡΑΓΓΑΟΝΟΜ). Translation: abyss (or ravine) of Onom

- Aleppo Codex: gy vn hnm (גי בן הנם). Translation: Valley of the sons of Hnm

- Leningrad Codex: gei ven-Hinnom (גֵּי בֶן־הִנֹּם). Translation: Valley of the sons of Hinnom

- Targum Jerusalem: lecheilat bar Hinom (לְחֵילַת בַּר הִנֹם). Translation: the stength of the sons of Hinom

The Septuagint includes a different name in chapter 18, reading 'Forest of Sonnam' (ναπης Σονναμ) where the Masoretic text reads Valley of the Sons of Hinnom (גֵּי בֶן־הִנֹּם). The misreading of an H (𐤄) for a S (𐤔) indicates a transcription error when a Samaritan or Judahite version of the book was translated into Aramaic, however, the substitution of 'forest' for 'valley of the sons...' is clearly not a translation error. The combination of 'valley/abyss' and 'forest' suggests it is a reference to a gravesite, and not a physical valley. At the time, Canaanites marked gravesites by planting trees, usually oak, which was known as the 'Asherah' tree, because it could self-pollinate, and was therefore seen as a 'virgin' tree.

The origin of the word is likely a plural of hinn (حِنّ), a reference to an ancient extinct type of being that once lived on the Earth in Semitic folklore. The hinns continue to be part of the Islamic and Druze religions, although their roles in the religions vary. It is agreed that they are extinct, however, it isn't clear what they were. Many sources describe the hinn and binn as powerful, gigantic primordial creatures, suggesting they were influenced by finding the bones of extinct animals. Conversely, the Revelations of 'Abdullah Al-Sayid Muhammad Habib claims the hinns were air creatures, and their enemies the binns were water creatures, while the medieval Islamic historian al-Tabari claimed they were created from poisonous fire (سموم). In most versions of the stories, they fought in part of a series of wars for control of the earth before the creation of humanity, and most of the ancient species became extinct, including the hinns.

In the context of a gravesite, it is likely that the term 'sons of hinns' did not refer to some known people, but an ancient gravesite of a by then unknown people. Oak trees are known to live over 1000 years, and reproduce, so the gravesite in question could have already been thousands of years old. Later during the reforms of King Josiah, ancient graves and Asherah groves near Jerusalem were destroyed, and he was specifically recorded as destroying a statue in the valley of the sons of Hinns, implying that this was the gravesite he destroyed.

3 Codex Vaticanus: Dabir an to proteron Polis grammatôn (ΔΑΒΙΡ ΗΝ ΤΟ ΠΡΟΤΕΡΟΝ ΠΟΛΙϹ ΓΡΑΜΜΑΤѠΝ). Translation: Dabir it was previously City of Letters (or writing)

- Aleppo Codex: dbr lpnym qryt spr (**דבר לפנים קרית ספר**). Translation: Dbr was formerly Village Book (or scroll)

- Leningrad Codex: dəbir lefanim kiryat-sefer (דְּבִר לְפָנִים קִרְיַת־סֵפֶר). Translation: Debir was formerly Village of Book (or scroll)

- Targum Jerusalem: dəbar milkadmin kiryat archei (דְבַר מִלְקַדְמִין קִרְיַת אַרְכֵי). Translation: Debar was in old days village of chief

The location of this city is unclear, however, it is often identified with Khirbet Rabud in the West Bank of Palestinian Territories.

4 Codex Vaticanus: thalassa ê megalê (ΘΑΛΑϹϹΑΗ ΜΕΓΑΛΗ). Translation: sea the great

- Aleppo Codex: hym hgbwl [hgdwl] (הים הגבול [הגדול]). Translation: sea the edge [the great]

- Leningrad Codex: hayyam haggavovl K [haggadovl Q] (הַיָּם הַגְּבוֹל כ [הַגָּדוֹל ק]). Translation: sea the edge (K) [the great (Q)]

- Targum Jerusalem: yama Rabbah (יְמָא רַבָּה). Translation: sea great

The Great Sea was a name for the Mediterranean.

5 Codex Vaticanus: polis grammatôn autê estin Dabir (ΠΟΛΙϹ ΓΡΑΜΜΑΤΩΝ ΑΥΤΗ ΕϹΤΙΝ ΔΑΒΙΡ). Translation: city of letters this is Dabir

- Codex Alexandrinus: Polis grammatôn hautê Dabir (ΠΟΛΙϹ ΓΡΑΜΜΑΤΩΝ ΑΥΤΗ ΔΑΒΙΡ). Translation: city of letters it's Dabir

- Aleppo Codex: qryt snh hyå dbr (קרית סנה היא דבר). Translation: village of bush (or bramble) it is Debir

- Leningrad Codex: kiryat-sannah hi devir (קִרְיַת־סַנָּה הִיא דְבִר). Translation: village of bush (or bramble) it is Debir

- Targum Jerusalem: kiryat sanah hi devir (קְרְיַת סַנָה הִיא דְבִיר). Translation: village of bush (or bramble) it's Debir

Chapter 16

The borders of the children of Joseph were from the Jordan by Jericho to the east, and they went up from Jericho to the hill country, to the wilderness, to the Temple of El in Luza,[1] and they will go out to the Temple of El and continue to the borders of the Archites. They go across to the sea to the borders of Japhletites, as far as the borders of Lower House of Horon, and from there the border will be the sea. The sons of Joseph, Ephraim, and Manasseh took their inheritance.

The borders of the children of Ephraim were according to their families, and the borders of their inheritance were to the east of Ataroth, and Eroc as far as Upper House of Horon, and Gazara. The borders continue to the sea to Icasmon north of Therma, and they go east to Taanath and Sellesa and pass on eastward to Janohah, and to Macho, and Ataroth, these are their villages, and they will come to Jericho and will start at Jordan. The borders will proceed from Tappuah to the sea by Kanah, and the end will be at the sea. This is the inheritance of the tribe of Ephraim according to their families.

The cities separated to the Ephramites were among the inheritance of the sons of Manasseh, all the cities and their villages. Ephraim did not destroy the Canaanites who lived in Gezer, and the Canaanites lived in Ephraim until Pharaoh the king of Egypt went up and took it, and burnt it with fire. The Canaanites and Perizzite, and the residents in Gaza were destroyed, and Pharaoh gave them as a dowry to his daughter.

Chapter 16 Notes

1 Codex Vaticanus: Baethêl Louza (ⲃⲀⲓⲐⲏⲗⲟⲨⲌⲀ)

- Aleppo Codex: Byt Ål lwzh (**בית אל לוזה**). Translation: House (or Temple) of El (or God) in Luza

- Leningrad Codex: Veit-Ēl lûzâ (בֵּית־אֵל לוּזָה). Translation: House (or Temple) of El (or God) in Luza

- Targum Jerusalem: Veit Ēl (בֵּית אֵל). Translation: House (or Temple) of El

Chapter 17

The borders of the tribe of the children of Manasseh, (as he was the firstborn of Joseph,) assigned to Machir the firstborn of Manasseh the father of Gilead, as he was a warrior, were the lands of Gilead and of Bashan. There was land assigned to the other sons of Manasseh according to their families. To the sons of Jezi and to the sons of Kelez, and to the sons of Asriel, and to the sons of Shechem, and to the sons of Symarim, and to the sons of Hepher, these are the males according to their families.

Zelophehad the sons of Hepher had no sons but daughters, and these are the names of the daughters of Zelophehad: Maala, Noah, Hoglah, Milcah, and Tirzah. They stood before Eleazar the priest, and before Joshua, and before the rulers, and said, "God gave an order by the hand of Moses, to give us an inheritance among our brothers," so there was given to them by the command of the Lord an inheritance among the brothers of their father. Their lot fell to them from Manasseh, and to the plain of Labec of the land of Gilead, which is beyond Jordan. For the daughters of the sons of Manasseh inherited a portion among their brothers, and the land of Gilead was assigned to the remainder of the sons of Manasseh.

The borders of the sons of Manasseh were Delanath, which was before the sons of Anath, and it proceeded to the borders even to Jamin and Jassib to the Fountain of Tappuah. It belonged to Manasseh, and Tappuah on the borders of Manasseh belonged to the Ephramites. The borders went down to the valley of Kanah southward by the valley of Jezreel (there is a turpentine tree belonging to Ephraim between that and the city of Manasseh), and the borders of Manasseh are north to the brook, and the sea will be its end. To the south, the land belonged to Ephraim, and north to Manasseh and the sea was their border. To the north, they bordered Asher, and to the east Issachar.

Manasseh had in the portion of Issachar: Asher, the House of Shean and their villages, and the inhabitants of Dor, and its villages, and the inhabitants of Megiddo, and its villages, and the third part of Mapheta, and its villages. The sons of Manasseh were not able to destroy these cities, and the Canaanites began to live in that land. It happened that when the Israelites were strong, they made the Canaanites subject, but they did not completely destroy them. The sons of Joseph asked Joshua, "Why have you caused us to inherit one inheritance and one line? We are a great people, and God has blessed us."

Joshua replied to them, "If you are a great people, go up to the forest, and clear the land for yourself, if Mount Ephraim is too little for you."

CHAPTER 17

They answered, "Mount Ephraim does not please us, and the Canaanites living in it in the House of Shean, and in its villages, and in the valley of Jezrael, have the best cavalry and iron."

Joshua said to the sons of Joseph, "If you are a great people, and have great strength, you will not have only one inheritance. For you have the wood, for there is a forest and you will clear it, ard the land will be yours. Then you will completely destroy the Canaanites, for they have the best cavalry, yet you are stronger."

Chapter 18

All the congregation of the Israelites was assembled at Shiloh, and there they pitched the tabernacle of witness, and the land was subdued by them. The sons of Israel remained, all those who had not received their inheritance, seven tribes.

Joshua said to the sons of Israel, "How long will you wait to inherit the land that Lord the god has given you? Appoint for yourselves three men from each tribe, and let them rise up and go through the land, and let them describe it to me, as it would be best to divide it. They came to him and he divided to them seven portions, saying, "Judah will be for them a southern border, and the sons of Joseph will be for them a northern border. Divide the land into seven parts, and bring the description here to me, and I will bring your lot before Lord the god. The Levites have no part among you, for the priesthood of the Lord is his portion. Gad, Reuben, and the half-tribe of Manasseh have received their inheritance beyond the Jordan to the east, which Moses the servant of the Lord gave to them.

The men rose and went out, and Joshua ordered the men who went to walk through the land, saying, "Go and explore the land and come to me, and I will bring your lot here before the Lord in Shiloh."

They went and explored the land, and they viewed
it, and described it according to the cities, seven parts in a
book, and brought the book to Joshua. Joshua cast the lot
for them in Shiloh before the Lord. The lot of the tribe of
Benjamin came out first according to their families, and
the borders of their lot came out between the children of
Judah and the children of Joseph. Their borders were to
the north from the Jordan near Jericho to the mountain
in the west, and the start of it will be the Temple of An[1]
of the desert-dwellers.[2]

The borders will go out there to Luz, to the south of
Luz, (this is the Temple of El). The borders will go
down to Ataroth Addar, to the hill country, which is
southward of Lower House of Horon. The borders will
pass through and proceed to the part that looks towards
the sea, on the south, from the mountain in front of
House of Horon southward, and its termination will be at
the town of Ba'al, this is the town of Jearim, a city of the
children of Judah towards the west.

The south side on the part of the town of Ba'al and the
borders will go across to Gasin, to the fountain of the
water of Nephtoah. The borders will extend down on
one side, this is in front of the Forest of Hinns[3] (which is
the Valley of Raphites of the north),[4] and go down the
Valley of Hinns[5] south of the Jebusites. It will come
down to the Fountain of Rogel. The borders will go

across to the Fountain of the Temple of Shemesh, and will proceed to Geliloth, which is on the way to Adummim, and they will come down to the stone of Bohan of the sons of Reuben, and will pass to the north of the House of Arabah, and will go down to the borders to the north of the sea. The termination of the borders will be at the creek of the salt sea northward to the south side of the Jordan. These are their southern borders. The Jordan will be their boundary on the east. This is the inheritance of the children of Benjamin, these are their borders according to their families.

The cities of the children of Benjamin according to their families were Jericho, the House of Hoglah, the Valley of Keziz, the House of Arabah, Sarai, Besana, Avim, Phara, Ophrah, Carapha, Cephira, Moni, Geba; twelve cities and their villages.

Gibeon, Ramah, Beeroth, Mizpah, Miron, Amoke, Phira, Caphan, Nacan, Selecan, Taralah, Jebus (this is Jerusalem), Gibeah; thirteen cities, and their villages.

This is the inheritance of the sons of Benjamin according to their families.

Chapter 18 Notes

1 Codex Vaticanus: Baethôn (ʙʌɪѳѡɴ)

- Aleppo Codex: Byt Åwn (**בית און**)

- Leningrad Codex: Veit Aven (בֵּית אָוֶן)

- Targum Jerusalem: Veit Aven (בֵּית אָוֶן)

The Temple of Ôn / Aven was still being used in the time of Hosea, in the 700s BC, as he warned Israelites not to worship there. On was also the name of Moses' god in the Septuagint's book of Exodus, which claims that Ôn (Ὤν) was the name that he was known to by Abram, Isaac, and Jacob. This implies that the original name of Abram's god was Anu (✳), the Mesopotamian version of El, which would support his origin story in the city of Ur.

2 Codex Vaticanus: Madbaritis (ΜΑΔΒΑΡΙΤΙϹ). Translation: Madbarites

- Aleppo Codex: mdbr (**מדבר**). Translation: desert (or wilderness)

- Leningrad Codex: midbara (מִדְבָּר). Translation: desert (or wilderness)

- Targum Jerusalem: madbar (מַדְבַּר). Translation: desert (or wilderness)

Similar to the transliteration of Madbaritidi (Μαδβαρῖτις) in chapter 5, this a synthesis of the Aramaic mdbrå (ܐܪܒܕܡ) meaning 'desert' and the Greek '-itis' (-ῖτις), meaning 'people of,' the precursor to the modern English '-ites.' Again, the Greek appears to have translated the Aramaic word mdbråyn (𐤔𐤀𐤉𐤃𐤓𐤒), meaning 'desert-dweller,' which is a deviation from the simpler term 'desert' found in the Hebrew and Judeo-Aramaic translations. The deviation likely occurred because the term desert-dwellers could be a reference to the Israelites themselves during the era, and the Hebrew translators wanted to clarify that it was a temple in the desert, not the temple in Samaria.

3 Codex Vaticanus: napês Sonnam (ΝΑΠΗϹϹΟΝΝΑΜ).
Translation: woodland (or grove) of Sonnam

- Aleppo Codex: gy vn hnm (גֵי בֶן הִנֹם). Translation: Valley of the sons of Hnm

- Leningrad Codex: gei ven-Hinnom (גֵי בֶן־הִנֹּם).
Translation: Valley of the sons of Hinnom

- Targum Jerusalem: cheilat bar Hinom (חֵילַת בַּר הִנֹם).
Translation: stength of the sons of Hinom

The Septuagint includes a different name in chapter 18, reading 'abyss of Onom' (φαραγγα ονομ) where the Masoretic text reads Valley of the Sons of Hinnom (גֵי בֶן־הִנֹּם), indicating the Aramaic translation used shorter names than the Judahite and Samaritan versions. The difference between in the names Sonnam and Hinnom in this verse likely originated when the Aramaic translation was created, as the Canaanite's script, which was used for Samaritan and Judahite in the early iron age, had similar shapes for the H (𐤄) and the Ś (𐤎). While the

CHAPTER 18 NOTES

Aramaic script did not have a similar H (𝑇) and Ś (𝑌), the early Greek alphabet did have a similar H (ϵ) and Š (ϲ), and therefore, the error could be interpreted as a Greek copying error. However, a virtually identical error is found in the Judahite Apocalypse of Ezra, which rendered the Sea of Edom as the Sea of Sodom. In that case, it was the word 'the/of' in between 'sea' and 'Edom' that was misread as an S, indicating the error took place in the Canaanite script.

The origin of the name Hnm (הנם) is likely a plural of hinn (حنّ), a reference to an ancient extinct type of being that once lived on the Earth in Semitic folklore. The hinns continue to be part of the Islamic and Druze religions, although their roles in the religions vary. It is agreed that they are extinct, however, it isn't clear what they were. Many sources describe the hinns and binns as powerful, gigantic primordial creatures, suggesting they were influenced by finding the bones of extinct animals. Conversely, the Revelations of 'Abdullah Al-Sayid Muhammad Habib claims the hinns were air creatures, and the binns were water creatures, while the medieval Islamic historian al-Tabari claimed they were created from poisonous fire (سموم). In most versions of the stories, they fought in part of a series of wars for control of the earth before the creation of humanity, and most of the ancient species became extinct, including the hinns.

The substitution of 'forest' or 'woodland' for 'valley of the sons...' is clearly not a translation error. The combination of 'valley/abyss' and 'forest/woodland' suggests it is a reference to a gravesite, and not a physical valley. At the time,

Canaanites marked gravesites by planting trees, usually oak, which was known as the 'Asherah' tree, because it could self-pollinate, and was therefore seen as a 'virgin' tree. In the context of a gravesite, it is likely that the term 'sons of hinns' did not refer to some known people, but an ancient gravesite of a by then unknown people. Oak trees are known to live over 1000 years, and reproduce, so the gravesite in question could have already been thousands of years old. Later during the reforms of King Josiah, ancient graves and Asherah groves near Jerusalem were destroyed, and he was specifically recorded as destroying a statue in the valley of the sons of Hinns, implying that this was the gravesite he destroyed.

4 Codex Vaticanus: merous Emecraphaen apo borrha (ΜΕΡΟΥⲤ ΕΜΕΚΡΑΦΑΕΙΝ ΑΠΟ ΒΟΡΡΑ). Translation: region of Emecraphaen of the north

- Aleppo Codex: åshr vômk rfåm tzfvnh (אשר בעמק רפאים צפונה). Translation: exists the valley of Raphaim northern

- Leningrad Codex: asher be'emek refa'im tzafovnah (אֲשֶׁר בְּעֵמֶק רְפָאִים צָפוֹנָה). Translation: exists the valley Raphaim northern

- Targum Jerusalem: bemeishar gibbaraya tzifuna (בְּמֵישַׁר גִּבָּרַיָּא צָפוּנָא). Translation: straight of the husband of the north

As the Greek includes a transliteration of the Hebrew, the Hebrew is imported. This scribal note seems to confirm that the 'Forest of Hinns' was the 'valley of the Raphiam,' supporting the term 'valley/abyss of hinns' referring to a graveyard. The two terms translated as 'Hinns' and 'Raphites' are not generally found in the same ancient literature, with hinns being mostly found in Arabic literature, and Raphites being mostly found in Canaanite literature.

This scribal note, in both the Greek and Hebrew translations, indicates the scribe was trying to let a northern reader understand that a Hinn was a Raphite. This shows that the original language of the text was more influenced by Arabic than Canaanite, supporting the claims that the people following Joshua had previously been in the Arabian desert. The scribal note must date back to an earlier copy of the text, as there would have been no reason to add it to both the Aramaic and Judahite translations, which later served as the basis for the Greek and Hebrew. The Aramaic translators would have simply used the correct Aramaic term, and left the Judahite text unaltered. It probably originated in the Samaritan version of the text, as at its height, the Kingdom of Israel was reported to have spanned the Levant from Edom to Hama.

At other points in the Septuagint, the Valley of Raphim is translated as the Valley of Gigantes (κοιλαδι των γιγαντων), indicating that the Greeks were not clear on who the sons of the Raphim were. It is likely that this was not being used as a reference to a tribe by the time the scribal note was added, as the Raphites (𐤓𐤐𐤀) were already viewed as residing in the underworld in Ugaritic Texts from the mid-1300s BC.

5 Codex Vaticanus: Gaeenna (ⲅⲁⲓⲉⲛⲛⲁ). Translation: Gaeenna

- Aleppo Codex: gy hnm (גי הנם). Translation: valley Hnm

- Leningrad Codex: gei Hinnom (גֵּי הִנֹּם). Translation: valley Hinnom

- Targum Jerusalem: lecheilat bar hinom (לְחֵילַת בַּר הִנֹם). Translation: the army (or strength, force) of the sons of Hinom

As the Greek includes a transliteration of the Hebrew 'valley of Hinns,' the Hebrew is imported.

Chapter 19

The second lot came out for the children of Simeon, and their inheritance was in the middle of the lots of the children of Judah. Their lot was Beersheba, Sheba, Caladam, Arsola, Balah, Jason, Erthula, the Temple of El, Hormah, Ziklag, the House of Marcaboth, the Yard of Susah, the House of Lebaoth, and their fields; thirteen cities, and their villages.

Rimmon, Thalcha, Jetheth, and Ashan; four cities and their villages around the cities as far as Balec as men go south to Bameth.

This is the inheritance of the tribe of the children of Simeon according to their families. The inheritance of the tribe of the children of Simeon was a part of the lot of Judah, for the portion of the children of Judah was greater than theirs, and the children of Simeon inherited in the middle of their lot.

The third lot came out to Zebulun according to their families. The borders of their inheritance will be: Esedekgola will be their border, the sea, and Magelda, and it will reach towards the House of Arabah in the valley, which is opposite Jokneam. The border returned from Sedduc in a contrary direction eastward from the Temple of Shemesh, to the borders of Chisloth Tabor, and will pass on to Daberath, and will proceed upward to Phangai. There it will come around in the opposite direction eastward to Gebere to the city of Kazin, and will go on to Rimmon Ammatharim Annoua.[1] The borders will come north to Hannathon, and will continue on to Jiphthah El, Kattath, Nahalal, Shimron, Jericho, and the House of Lehem. This is the inheritance of the tribe of the sons of Zebulun according to their families, these cities and their villages.

The fourth lot came out to Issachar. Their borders were Jezreel, Chesulloth, Shunem, Agin, Shion, Reeroth, Anaharath, Dabiron, Kishion, Abez, Remeth, Jeon, Tomman, Aemarec, and Bersaphes. The boundaries will border on Gaethbor, and on Salim westward, and the Temple of Shemesh, and the extremity of his border will be the Jordan. This is the inheritance of the tribe of the children of Issachar according to their families, the cities and their villages.

The fifth lot came out to Asher according to their families. Their borders were Helkath, Hali, Bathok, Achshaph, Alammelech, Ammi-El, and Maasa, and the lot bordered on Carmel in the west, and on Sihon and Libnath. It will return westward from the Temple of Dagon, and will join Zebulun and the valley of Iphtah-El to the north, and the borders will come to the north Beth Emek, and Neiel, and will go on to Cabul on the left, including Ebron, Rehob, Hammon, and Kanah to Sidon the Great. The borders will turn back to Ramah, and to the Fountain of Masphassat, and the Tyrians and the borders will return to Hosah, and their end will be the sea by Apoleb, Achzib, Archob, Aphek, and Rehob. This is the inheritance of the tribe of the sons of Asher according to their families, the cities and their villages.

The sixth lot came out to Naphtali. Their borders were Moolam, Mola, Besemiin, Arme, Nekeb, Jeph-thamai, as far as Dodam, and ended at the Jordan. The coasts returned westward by Athabor, and go out from there to Jacana, and border on Zebulun to the south, and Asher will join it to the west, and the Jordan to the east. The walled cities of the Tyrians: Tyre, Omathadaketh, Kenereth, Armaith, Areal, Hazor, Kadesh, Assari, the well of Hazor, Iron, Migdal El, the Temple of Anath, and the Temple of Shemesh. This is the inheritance of the tribe of the children of Naphtali.

The seventh lot came out to Dan. Their borders were Zorah, Asa, the City of Shemesh, Salamin, Ammon, Jethlah, Elon, Timnah, Ekron, Eltekeh, Begethon, and Gebeelan, Azor, Bene-berak, and Gath Rimmon. West of Hieracon the border was near to Jaffa. This is the inheritance of the tribe of the children of Dan, according to their families, these are their cities and their villages.

The children of Dan did not drive out the Amorites who attacked them in the mountains, and the Amorites would not allow them to come down into the valley, but they forcibly took from them the border of their portion. The sons of Dan went and fought against Leshem, and took it, and slaughtered it with the edge of the sword, and they lived in it and called the name of it Leshem Dan. The Amorites continued to live in Edom and in Salamin, and the hand of Ephraim prevailed against them, and they became a tribute for them.

They proceeded to take possession of the land according to their borders, and the Israelites gave an inheritance to Joshua the son of Nun among them, by the command of God, and they gave him the city which he asked for, Timnath Serah, which is on Mount Ephraim, and he built the city and lived in it. These are the divisions which Eleazar the priest divided by lot, and Joshua the son of Nun, and the heads of families among the tribes of Israel, according to the lots, in Shiloh before the Lord by the doors of the tabernacle of testimony, and they went to take possession of the land.

Chapter 19 Notes

1 Codex Vaticanus: Remmôn Ammatharim Annoua (ⲣⲉⲙⲙⲱⲛⲁⲙⲙⲁⲑⲁⲣⲓⲙⲁⲛⲛⲟⲩⲁ)

- Aleppo Codex: Rmwn hmtår hnôh (**רמון המתאר הנעה**)

- Leningrad Codex: Rimmovn hammeto'ar hanne'ah (רִמּוֹן הַמְּתֹאָר הַנֵּעָה)

- Targum Jerusalem: Rimon dimto'ar umittaman mistechar lene'ah (רמוֹן דְּמְתוֹאַר וּמִתַּמָן מִסְתְּחַר לְנֵעָה). Translation: desert (or wilderness)

In this case, the Greeks transliterated a word similar to hammeto'ar (הַמְּתֹאָר) as Ammatharim (Αμμαθαριμ). As 'hammesoor' translates as 'that describes' it is possible that the text originated by the scribal note "(which is Annoua)" however, that cannot be known for sure. As it is, neither the Greek nor Hebrew translations make sense in this verse.

Chapter 20

The Lord said to Joshua, "Tell the Israelites, 'Assign the cities of refuge, of which I told you through Moses. A refuge for the slayer who has struck a man unintentionally. The cities will be refuges for you, and the slayer will not be put to death by the avenger of blood until he has stood before the congregation for judgment.'"

Joshua separated Kadesh in Galilee on Mount Naphtali, and Shechem on Mount Ephraim, and the city of Arba (this is Hebron), in the mountains of Judah. Beyond the Jordan, he appointed Bezer in the wilderness in the plain out of the tribe of Reuben, and Ramoth in Gilead out of the tribe of Gad, and Golan in the country of Bashan out of the tribe of Manasseh.

These were the cities selected for the sons of Israel, and for the stranger living among them, that everyone who kills a mind unintentionally should flee there, that he should not die by the hand of the avenger of blood until he should stand before the congregation for judgment.

Chapter 21

The heads of the families of the Levites approached Eleazar the priest and Joshua the son of Nun, and to the heads of families of the tribes of Israel. They said to them in Shiloh in the land of Canaan, "The Lord gave commandment by Moses to give us cities to live in, and the country around it for our livestock."

The Israelites gave the Levites their inheritance by the command of the Lord, the cities, and the country around them. The lot came out for the Kohathites, and the sons of Aaron, the priests the Levites, had by lot thirteen cities out of the tribes of Judah, Simeon, and Benjamin. To the sons of Kohath that were left were given by lot ten cities, out of the tribes of Ephraim and Dan, and out of the half-tribe of Manasseh. The sons of Gershon had thirteen cities, out of the tribes of Issachar, Asher, Naphtali, and out of the half-tribe of Manasseh in the land of Bashan. The sons of Merari according to their families had by lot twelve cities, out of the tribes of Reuben, Gad, and Zebulun. The Israelites gave to the Levites the cities and their suburbs by lot, as the Lord commanded Moses. The tribe of the children of Judah, and the children of Simeon, and part of the tribe of the children of Benjamin gave these cities, and they were assigned to the sons of Aaron of the family of Kohath of the Levites, for the lot fell to these. And they gave to them the town of Arba, the mother-city of the sons of

Anaks (this is Hebron), in the mountainous country of Judah, and the suburbs around it. But the lands of the city and its villages Joshua gave to the sons of Caleb the son of Jephunneh for a possession. To the sons of Aaron, he gave the city of refuge for the slayer, Hebron, and the suburbs belonging to it, and Libnah, and the suburbs belonging to it, and Elon and its suburbs, and Teman and its suburbs, Gella and its suburbs, and Debir and its suburbs, and Asa and its suburbs, and Tany and its suburbs, and the Temple of Shemesh and its suburbs; nine cities from these two tribes.

From the tribe of Benjamin, Gibeon and its suburbs, Geba and its suburbs, Anathoth and its suburbs, Almon and its suburbs; four cities. All the cities of the sons of Aaron the priests, thirteen. To the families, including the sons of Kohath the Levites, that were left of the sons of Kohath, there was given their priests' city, out of the tribe of Ephraim, and they gave them the slayer's city of refuge Shechem, and its suburbs, and Gezer and its suburbs, and House of Horon and its suburbs; four cities. From the tribe of Dan: Eltekeh and its suburbs, Gibbethon and its suburbs, Ayalon and its suburbs, Gath Rimmon and its suburbs; four cities.

Out of the half-tribe of Manasseh: Taanach and its suburbs, and Jebatha and its suburbs; two cities. In all were given ten cities, and the suburbs of each belonging to them, to the families of the sons of Kohath that remained. Joshua gave to the sons of Gershon the Levites out of the other half-tribe of Manasseh cities set apart for the slayers, Golan in the country of Bashan, and its suburbs, and Bosora and its suburbs; two cities.

Out of the tribe of Issachar: Kishion and its suburbs, Daberath and its suburbs, Remmath and its suburbs, and the Well of Letters, and its suburbs; four cities.

Out of the tribe of Asher: Basella and its suburbs, and Abdon and its suburbs, and Helkath and its suburbs, and Rehob and its suburbs; four cities.

Of the tribe of Naphtali: the city set apart for the slayer, Kadesh in Galilee, and its suburbs, and Hammoth Dor, and its suburbs; and Themmon and its suburbs; three cities. All the cities of the Gershonites according to their families were thirteen cities. To the family of the sons of Merari the Levites that remained, he gave out of the tribe of Zebulun, Mahanaim and its suburbs, Kadesh and its suburbs, and Zillah and its suburbs: three cities.

Beyond the Jordan near Jericho, out of the tribe of Reuben: the city of refuge for the slayer, Bezer in the wilderness, Miso and its suburbs, Jahaz and its suburbs, Kedemoth and its suburbs, Mephaath and its suburbs; four cities.

CHAPTER 21

Out of the tribe of Gad the city of refuge for the slayer, both Ramoth in Gilead, and its suburbs, Mahanaim and its suburbs, Heshbon and its suburbs, Jazer and its suburbs: the cities were four in all. All these cities were given to the sons of Merari according to the families of them that were left out of the tribe of Levi, and their limits were the twelve cities. All the cities of the Levites among the possession of the Israelites, were forty-eight cities, and their suburbs around these cities, a city and the suburbs round about the city to all these cities: and Joshua ceased dividing the land by their borders: and the Israelites gave a portion to Joshua because of the commandment of the Lord: they gave him the city which he asked: they gave him Timnath Serah on Mount Ephraim, and Joshua built the city and lived in it. Joshua took the knives of stone, which he circumcised the Israelites that were born in the desert along the way, and put them in Timnath Serah. So the Lord gave to Israel all the land which he swore to give to their fathers: and they inherited it, and lived in it. The Lord gave them the rest around at, as he swore to their fathers: not one of all their enemies maintained his ground against them. The Lord delivered all their enemies into their hands. Not one of the good things which the Lord said to the Israelites failed. All happened.

Chapter 22

Then Joshua called together the sons of Reuben, and the sons of Gad, and the half-tribe of Manasseh, and said to them, "You have heard all that Moses the servant of the Lord commanded you, and you have listened to my voice in all that he commanded you. You have not deserted your brothers these many days. Until this day you have kept the commandment of Lord the god. Now Lord the god has given our brothers rest, as he told them. Now then, return and leave to your homes, and to the land of your possession, which Moses gave you on the other side of the Jordan. But take great heed to do the commands and the law, which Moses the servant of the Lord commanded you to do: to love Lord the god, to walk in all his ways, to keep his commands, and to cling to him, and serve him with all your mind, and with all your mind."

Joshua blessed them and dismissed them, and they went to their homes. To one half of the tribe of Manasseh Moses gave a portion in the land of Bashan, and to the other half, Joshua gave a portion with his brothers on the west side of the Jordan. When Joshua sent them away to their homes, then he blessed them. They departed with much wealth to their houses, and they divided the spoil of their enemies with their brothers, a great deal of live-stock, silver, gold, iron, and many clothes. So the sons of Reuben, and the sons of Gad, and the half-tribe of

Manasseh, departed from the Israelites in Shiloh in the land of Canaan, to go away into Gilead, into the land of their possession, which they inherited by the command of the Lord, by the hand of Moses.

They came to Gilead of Jordan, which is in the land of Canaan. The children of Reuben, and the children of Gad, and the half-tribe of Manasseh built an altar there by the Jordan, a great altar to look at. The Israelites were heard to say, "Look, the sons of Reuben, Gad, and the half-tribe of Manasseh have built an altar at the borders of the land of Canaan at Gilead of Jordan, on the opposite side as the Israelites." All the Israelites gathered together to Shiloh, to go up and fight against them. The Israelites sent to the sons of Reuben, Gad, and the half-tribe of Manasseh in the land of Gilead, both Phinehas the son of Eleazar the son of Aaron the priest, and ten of the chiefs with him, one chief of every household out of all the tribes of Israel, (the heads of families are the captains of thousands in Israel.)

They came to the sons of Reuben, Gad, and the half-tribe of Manasseh in the land of Gilead, and said to them, "The whole congregation of the Lord says, 'What is this transgression that you have done before the God of Israel, to turn away today from the Lord, in that you have built for yourselves an altar so that you should be apostates from the Lord? Is the sin of Peor too little for you, whereas we have not been cleansed from it until this day, though there was a plague among the congregation of the Lord? You have this day rebelled from the Lord. It will come to pass if you revolt this day from the Lord, that tomorrow there will be anger on all Israel."

"Now if the land of your possession is too little, cross over to the land of the possession of the Lord, where the tabernacle of the Lord lives, and receive your inheritance among us. Do not become apostates from God, neither become apostates from the Lord, because of your having built an altar apart from the altar of Lord the god. Look! did not Achan the son of Zerah commit a trespass taking of the cursed thing, and there was anger on the whole congregation of Israel? Yet he himself died alone in his own sin."

The sons of Reuben, Gad, and the half-tribe of Manasseh answered the captains of the thousands of Israel, "The god of gods is Lord, and the god of gods, Lord himself knows[1] and judges Israel. If we have transgressed before the Lord by apostasy, let him not save us this day. If we have built for ourselves an altar, to apostatize from Lord the god, to offer on it a sacrifice of whole burnt offerings, to offer on it a sacrifice of peace offering, the Lord will require it. But we have done this for the sake of precaution concerning this thing, saying, 'In case from now on your sons should say to our sons, 'What

have you to do with Lord the god of Israel? The Lord
has set boundaries between us and you, even the Jordan,
and you have no portion in the Lord,' and your sons will
alienate our sons, that they should not worship the
Lord.'"

"We gave orders to do this, to build this altar, not for
burnt offerings, nor for meat-offerings, but that this may
be a witness between you and us, and between our
posterity after us, that we may do service to the Lord
before him, with our burnt offerings and our meat-offerings and our peace offerings. So your sons will not say to
our sons, from now on, 'You have no portion in the
Lord.' We said, 'If ever it should come to pass that they
should speak so to us, or to our posterity from now on,
then will they say, 'Look the likeness of the altar of the
Lord, which our fathers made, not for the sake of burnt
offerings, nor for the sake of meat-offerings, but it is a
witness between you and us, and between our sons.' Far
be it from us therefore that we should turn away from
the Lord this day to apostatize from the Lord, so that we
should build an altar for burnt offerings, and for peace
offerings, besides the altar of the Lord which is before his
tabernacle."

Phinehas the priest and all the chiefs of the congregation of Israel who were with him heard the words
which the children of Reuben, Gad, and the half-tribe of

Manasseh spoke, and it pleased them. Phinehas the priest said to the sons of Reuben, Gad, and to the half-tribe of Manasseh, "Today we know that the Lord is with us, because you have not trespassed grievously against the Lord, and because you have delivered the Israelites out of the hand of the Lord."

So Phinehas the priest and the princes departed from the children of Reuben, Gad, and the half-tribe of Manasseh, out of Gilead to the land of Canaan to the Israelites, and reported the words to them. It pleased the Israelites, and they spoke to the Israelites, and blessed the God of the Israelites, and told them to not go up to war against the others and destroy the land of the children of Reuben, Gad, and the half-tribe of Manasseh. Joshua gave a name to the altar of the children of Reuben, Gad, and the half-tribe of Manasseh, and said, "It is a testimony among them, that the Lord is their God."

Chapter 22 Notes

1 Codex Vaticanus: o t̄h̄s t̄h̄s estin c̄s, cae o t̄h̄s t̄h̄s c̄s autòs oîden (OӨCOCЄCTINKCKAIOӨCOCKCAYTOCOIΔEN). Translation: the god god is lord, and the god god lord himself knows

• Aleppo Codex: ål ålhym yhwh ål ålhym yhwh hwå ydô (אל אלהים יהוה אל אלהים יהוה הוא ידע). Translation: the (or god, El) gods (or elohim) Yhwh the (or god, El) gods (or elohim) Yhwh he knows

• Leningrad Codex: el | elohim | Yehvah el | elohim | Yehvah hu yodea' (אֵל ׀ אֱלֹהִים ׀ יְהֹוָה אֵל ׀ אֱלֹהִים ׀ יְהֹוָה הֻוא ׀ יֹדֵעַ). Translation: god (or El) – gods (or elohim) – Yehwah god (or El) – gods (or elohim) – Yehwah he knows

• Targum Jerusalem: el elohim Yeyah el elohim Yeyah kodamohi yedia' (אֵל אֱלֹהִים יְיָ אֵל אֱלֹהִים יְיָ קֳדָמוֹהִי יְדִיעַ). Translation: god (or El) gods Yahw god (or El) gods Yahw he knows

As neither the Greek nor Hebrew text makes sense here, and clearly were not understood by the Masoretes due to their punctuation marks, it is assumed that the Greeks translated both 'el' and elohim as 'god,' as they did in other sections of the Septuagint. If the term elohim originally meant 'gods' in this verse, which is its Aramaic meaning, then the Aramaic precursor text would have read 'the god of gods is Lord (possibly Adonay or Ba'al), and the god of gods, Lord himself, knows..."

Chapter 23

Many days after the Lord had given Israel rest from all his enemies, when Joshua was old and advanced in years. Joshua called together all the Israelites, and their elders, and their chiefs, and their judges, and their officers, and said to them, "I am old and advanced in years. You have seen all that Lord the god has done to all these nations before us. It is Lord the god who has fought for you. See, that I have given to you these nations that are left to you by lots to your tribes, all the nations beginning at the Jordan. Some I have destroyed, and the boundaries will be at the great sea to the west."

"The Lord the god, will destroy them before us until they completely perish, and he will send against them the wild beasts until he has completely destroyed them and their kings from before you, and you will inherit their land, as Lord the god promised you. Therefore strive diligently to observe and do all things written in the book of the law of Moses, that you do not turn to the right or to the left, that you do not go in among these nations that are left, and the names of their gods will not be named among you. Neither will you serve them, neither will you bow down to them. But you will cling to Lord the god, as you have done until this day. The Lord will destroy them before you, even great and strong nations. No one has stood before us until this day.

CHAPTER 23

One of you has chased a thousand, because Lord the god, he fought for you, as he said to us."

"Pay close attention to love Lord the god. For if you will turn aside and attach yourselves to these nations that are left with you, and make marriages with them, and become mingled with them and they with you, know that the Lord will no longer destroy these nations from before you, and they will be to you snares and stumbling blocks, and nails in your heels, and darts in your eyes until you are destroyed from off this good land, which Lord the god has given you. But I quickly go the way of death, as all that are on the earth also do, and you know in your heart and in your mind, that not one word has fallen to the ground of all the words which Lord the god has spoken respecting all that concerns us".

"There has not one of them failed. It will come to pass, that as all the good things have come on us which Lord the god will bring on you all the evil things until he has destroyed you from off this good land, which the Lord has given you, when you transgress the covenant of Lord the god, which he has ordered us, and go and serve other gods, and bow down to them."

Chapter 24

Joshua gathered all the tribes of Israel to Shiloh, and assembled their elders, and their officers, and their judges, and set them before God. Joshua said to all the people, "Lord the god of Israel says, 'Your fathers at first stayed beyond the river, including Terah, the father of Abraham and the father of Nahor, and they served other gods. I took your father Abraham from the other side of the river, and I guided him through all the land, and I multiplied his seed, and I gave to him Isaac, and to Isaac Jacob and Esau. I gave to Esau Mount Seir for him to inherit, and Jacob and his sons went down to Egypt and became a great and populous and mighty nation there, and the Egyptians attacked them. I struck Egypt with the wonders that I worked among them.'"

"Afterward God brought out our fathers from Egypt, and you entered into the Papyrus Sea, and the Egyptians pursued after our fathers with chariots and horses into the Papyrus Sea. We cried aloud to the Lord, and he put a cloud and darkness between us and the Egyptians, and he brought the sea on them and covered them. Your eyes have seen all that the Lord did in the land of Egypt, and you were in the wilderness many days. He brought us into the land of the Amorites that lived beyond the Jordan, and the Lord delivered them into our hands, and you inherited their land, and completely destroyed them from before you. Balak, king of Moab, son of Zippor, rose, and made war against Israel, and sent and called Balaam to curse us. But Lord the god would not destroy you, and he greatly blessed us, and rescued us out of their hands, and delivered them to us. You crossed across the Jordan and came to Jericho, and the inhabitants of Jericho fought against us, the Amorites, Canaanites, Perizzites, Mitanni, Jebusites, Cypriots, and Girgasite, but the Lord delivered them into our hands. He sent out hornets before you, and he drove them out from before you, all twelve kings of the Amorites, not with your sword, nor with your bow."

"He gave you a land on which you did not labor and cities which you did not build, and you were settled in them. You eat of vineyards and olive yards which you did not plant. Now fear the Lord, and serve him in righteousness and justice, and remove the strange gods, which our fathers served beyond the river, and in Egypt, and serve the Lord. But if it does not seem good to you to serve the Lord, choose for yourselves today who you will serve, whether the gods of your fathers that were on the other side of the river, or the gods of the Amorites, among whose land you live in, but I and my house will serve the Lord, for he is holy."

The people answered and said, "Far be it from us to forsake the Lord, to serve other gods. Lord the god, he is God. He brought us and our fathers out from Egypt and protected us along the roads on which we walked, and among all the nations through which we passed. The Lord threw out the Amorites and all the nations that inhabited the land from before us. Yes, we will serve the Lord, for he is our god."

Joshua said to the people, "Indeed you will not be able to serve the Lord, for God is holy, and he being jealous will not forgive your sins and your transgressions. Whenever you will forsake the Lord and serve other gods, then he will come on you and afflict you, and consume you, because he has done good for you."

The people said to Joshua, "No, but we will serve the Lord."

Joshua said to the people, "You are witnesses against yourselves, that you have chosen the Lord to serve him. Now take away the strange gods that are among you, and set your heart right towards Lord the god of Israel."

The people replied to Joshua, "We will serve the Lord, and we will listen to his voice."

So Joshua made a covenant with the people on that day and gave them a law and an ordinance in Shiloh before the tabernacle of the God of Israel. He wrote these words in the book of the laws of God. Joshua took a great stone and set it up under the turpentine tree before the Lord. Joshua said to the people, "Look, this stone will be among you as a witness, for it has heard all the words that have been spoken to it by the Lord. He has spoken to you today, and this stone will be among you as a witness in the last days, whenever you will deal falsely with Lord the god."

Joshua dismissed the people, and they went every man to his place. It happened after these things that Joshua the son of Nun the servant of the Lord died, at the age of a hundred and ten years. They buried him by the borders of his inheritance in Timnath Serah on Mount Ephraim, north of Mount Gilead. There they put with him into the tomb in which they buried him, the knives of stone with which he circumcised the Israelites at the circle, when he brought them out of Egypt, as the Lord appointed them, and there they are to this day.

Israel served the Lord all the days of Joshua and all the days of the elders that lived as long as Joshua, and all that knew all the works of the Lord which he worked for Israel. The Israelites brought up the bones of Joseph out of Egypt, and buried them in Shechem, in the portion of the land which Jacob bought of the Amorites who lived in Shechem for a hundred ewe-lambs, and he gave it to Joseph for a portion. It happened afterward that Eleazar the high-priest the son of Aaron died and was buried in the hill of Phinehas his son, which he gave him on Mount Ephraim.

CHAPTER 24

On that day the Israelites took the box of God and carried it around among them, and Phinehas exercised the priest's office in place of Eleazar his father until he died, and he was buried in his own place Gabaar, but the Israelites departed every one to their place, and to their own city, and the Israelites worshiped Asherah and Astarte,[1] and the gods of the nations around them, and the Lord delivered them into the hands of Eglom king of Moab and he ruled over them eighteen years.[2]

Chapter 24 Notes

1 Codex Vaticanus: Astartên cae Astarôth (ΑϹΤΑΡΤΗΝΚΑΙ ΑϹΤΑΡѠѲ). Translation: Asherah and Astarte

This verse, is not found in the Masoretic Text. The two goddesses mentioned are the wives of El from the Ugaritic Texts: Åṯrt (𒀀𒊭𒅕), later called Asherah (אשרה) by the Israelites; and Ôṯtrt-ym (𒀀𒊭𒅕𒅎), later called Ôštrt (𐤏𐤔𐤕𐤓𐤕) by the Phoenicians, Astarte (Ἀστάρτη) by the Greeks, and Ashtoret (עַשְׁתֹּרֶת) by the Israelites. The names in the Septuagint are transliterations of the Aramaic names, not the Greek names, indicating that they were in the Aramaic version of Joshua. The more common English names are used.

2 This verse is not found in the Masoretic Text, indicating that the Septuagint's Joshua was made from a Samaritan text, and not a Judahite text, as Eglom king of Moab only conquered Gilead and Samaria, not Judah or Edom.

Septuagint Manuscripts

The following is a list of the Septuagint manuscripts referenced in the notes for this book.

LXX A (Codex Alexandrinus) is dated to the 5th century. It is currently located at the British Library (Royal 1 D. VIII) in London.

LXX B (Codex Vaticanus) is dated to the 4th century. It is currently located at the Vatican Library (Gr. 1209) in Vatican City.

Alternative Translations

The following is a list of alternative translations that were used for comparative analysis.

The Aleppo Codex is dated to circa 920 AD. For centuries it was housed at the Central Synagogue of Aleppo, from which its name is derived. It was the oldest known complete copy of the Hebrew scriptures used within Judaism until 1947, when it was seized and divided among Jewish families during anti-Jewish riots in Aleppo. The sections that have resurfaced are currently at the Israel Museum in Jerusalem. Approximately 40% is still missing.

The Leningrad Codex is dated to 1008 (or 1009) AD. It is currently located at the National Library of Russia (Firkovich B 19 A) in St. Petersburg. The Leningrad Codex is the oldest complete copy of the Hebrew scriptures used within Judaism.

Targum Jerusalem has historically been misidentified as the Targum Jonathan, and is commonly called the Targum Pseudo-Jonathan in academic literature. Its oldest name is the Targum Jerusalem, which is used here. It is written in Palestinian-Aramaic, and generally dated to sometime between the 4th and 11th centuries. Some scholars believe it originated in the 4th century, and was modified after the Islamic conquest of Palestine, as it includes some Arabic names generally found in Islamic sources. It existed before the crusades, as it was documented at the time.

Dead Sea Scrolls

The following is a list of the Dead Sea Scrolls mentioned in the notes for this book. Most are held by the Israel Museum in Jerusalem.

DSS 4Q47 (4QJosh[a]) is dated to the Herodian Dynasty in Judea (37 BC to 6 AD).

DSS 4Q48 (4QJosh[b]) is dated to the Herodian Dynasty in Judea (37 BC to 6 AD).

Also Available

ALSO AVAILABLE

- Octateuch: The Original Orit

ENOCH AND METATRON SERIES:
- Books of Enoch Collection

- Books of Enoch and Metatron Collection

- Books of Metatron Collection

- Secrets of Enoch

OTHER TRANSLATIONS:
- Apocalypses of Ezra

- Arabic Maccabees

- Life of Adam and Eve

- Memories of the New Kingdom

- Septuagint's Esther and the Vetus Latina Esther

- Septuagint's Ezekiel and the Ba'al Cycle

- Septuagint's Job and the Testament of Job

- Septuagint's Proverbs and the Wisdom of Amenemope

- The Amarna Letters

- Testaments of the Patriarchs Collection

- Tobit and Ahikar

- Ugaritic Texts: Ba'al Cycle

- Wisdom of Ahikar